THE STONEHENGE COMPANION

James McClintock

A THINK BOOK FOR

ENGLISH HERITAGE

What is Stonehenge? It is the roofless past;
Man's ruinous myth; his uninterred adoring
Of the unknown in sunrise cold and red;
His quest of stars that arch his doomed exploring.
Siegfried Sassoon, 'The Heart's Journey'

THINK
BOOKS

A Think Book
for English Heritage

First published in Great Britain in 2006 by
Think Publishing
The Pall Mall Deposit
124-128 Barlby Road, London W10 6BL
www.thinkpublishing.co.uk

Distributed in the United States and Canada by
Sterling Publishing Co., Inc.
387 Park Avenue South
New York, NY 10016-8810

Published in association with
English Heritage
Kemble Drive
Swindon SN2 2GZ

ENGLISH HERITAGE

Author: James McClintock
Companion team: Tania Adams, James Collins, Rica Dearman,
Emma Jones, Lou Millward, Matt Packer and Rob Turner
Cover illustration: Dominic Scott

ISBN-10 1-90562-408-5
ISBN-13 978-1-90562-408-9

Printed in Italy by 🌲 Grafica Veneta S.p.A.
The publishers and authors have made every effort to ensure the accuracy and
currency of the information in *The Stonehenge Companion*. Similarly, every
effort has been made to contact copyright holders. We apologise for any
unintentional errors or omissions. The publisher and authors disclaim any
liability, loss, injury or damage incurred as a consequence, directly or
indirectly, of the use and application of the contents of this book. The views
expressed by the author are not necessarily those of English Heritage.

*A pitch of architectural refinement
was achieved at Stonehenge unparalleled
in the prehistoric west.*
Jacquetta Hawkes, *Prehistoric Britain*

THANKS

This book wouldn't have been possible without the helpful input and expert knowledge of Rob Richardson and Julian Richards from English Heritage.

INTRODUCTION

The first man to record the existence of Stonehenge was Henry of
Huntingdon, a monkish chronicler who lived in the reign of Henry I.
'Stones,' he wrote, in giving a description of the most memorable
sights to be seen in the British Isles, 'of remarkable size are raised up
like gates, in such a way that gates seem to be placed on top of gates.'
Perhaps half a dozen years later, around 1136, his contemporary
Geoffrey of Monmouth also described the monument and offered the
earliest known explanation as to how the henge had been erected:
Merlin, Geoffrey wrote in his *History of the Kings of Britain*, had
brought the stones over from Ireland by magic, and re-erected them
in Wiltshire, using his 'wondrous art', at the behest of King Arthur.

Ever since Geoffrey's time, historians and archaeologists have
squabbled bitterly over the secrets of the stones. Who built the henge,
and when, and why? The vast literature on the subject offers dozens of
guesses, some more educated than others: Stonehenge was a Druid
temple, it is said, or an ancient clock, a place where the Saxons hanged
their British enemies, a computer, a tomb; and it was erected by the
Romans or the Danes, early Britons, Phoenicians, Atlanteans or even
(according to WS Blacket, author of *Researches Into the Lost Histories
of America* – 1883) by a band of American Indians who worshipped
the old Greek gods. 'One might almost suppose,' the antiquarian John
Michell wryly observes, 'that it was specially designed to accommodate
every notion that could possibly be projected onto it.'

The Stonehenge Companion, I am pleased to say, is a reliable guide to
all that is definitely known about the henge, and ably summarises not
merely the discoveries, but the controversies that have swirled around
this most celebrated of British monuments over the past millennia. It
digests every fact, and every figure, that visitors to Salisbury Plain
could possibly need to know. More than that, though, the *Companion*
clearly demonstrates that – whatever else Stonehenge may be – it serves
as a colossal mirror, reflecting the prejudices and preferences of each
passing age.

It seems to me that only two things are certain about grandest of all
megaliths. One, that it will outlast each one of us. And, two, that no
matter how much we think we know about the henge, the old stones
will go on tantalising and testing us, inspiring new theories and fresh
thinking in the years to come.

And that, of course, is just as things should be.

James McClintock, Editor

STONES WITHOUT NUMBER

Legend has it that the stones cannot be counted – each time you count you will obtain a different total. Which is just as well, because it was also believed during the eighteenth and nineteenth centuries that anyone who counted them correctly would die.

Noted naysayers who visited the site and did their sums include King Charles II (1 October 1651), who stated afterwards that 'Arthimetike gave the lye to that fabulous tale that those stones cannot be told alike twice together' and Samuel Pepys (11 June 1668) who declared in his famous *Diary* that 'they are hard to tell, but yet may be told'.

That said, many reporters claim to have counted the stones correctly, but have come up with wildly different numbers. Daniel Defoe, in 1724, reckoned there were 72, but 70 years before, John Evelyn had come up with 95 – either a great many had fallen down during the intervening period, or one of them was wrong. Still harder to countenance is an account from 1740, in which 68 more stones than Defoe sighted were apparently counted!

PETRIE'S RULES OF EXCAVATION

When William Flinders Petrie, the eminent Victorian archaeologist, heard of the decision to attempt to prop up Stonehenge following storm damage in 1900, he wrote to *The Times* with his own insights into how the matter should progress:

1. Not a handful of soil must be moved except under the instant inspection of a good archaeologist, who must live in a shed on the site. There must be no fooling about driving up each day from an hotel in Salisbury to find that workmen have wiped out historical evidences before breakfast.

2. The workmen must be trained hands, and full local value must be paid to them for everything they find; there must be no chance tales a year or two later about so and so having got prizes from the excavations.

3. A ground cut away in such measured slices that the place of every object is known to an inch.

4. The public must be kept out from all interference from the portion being worked, and no festive luncheons and notabilities must be allowed to distract the recorder for a moment.

SINNERS' DANCE

The Christian church has always been quick to borrow from the indigenous religions it supplanted. In Germanic mythology giants were supposed to turn to stone if they were so distracted by their night-time circle dances that they were caught in the open by the rays of the rising sun. This notion was quickly transformed into a punishment for dancing on the Sabbath. The alternative name for Stonehenge, *Chorea Gigantum*, or Giants' Dance, suggests that at some stage in its history locals believed the stones were a group of giants caught mid-jig. There's a similar stone ring in Prussia, also called Giants' Dance, which combines both legends and is supposed to be the petrified remains of a group of giants who preferred dancing to sitting in church on Sunday, and were punished for dancing during the Mass.

CASTING THE RUNES

Which of the following group of people have *not* been credited with
the building of Stonehenge?
a) American Indians
b) Martians
c) Brahmins
d) Australian Aboriginals
e) Phoenicians
Answer on page 153.

WHILE YOU'RE IN THE AREA WHY NOT VISIT...

Great Wishford

Located just off the A36 trunk road, a few miles from Salisbury, Great Wishford hosts an Oakapple Day fair called the Grovely Festival every 29 May, which supposedly commemorates the locals' victory in a squabble with landowner, the Earl of Pembroke. The Earl wanted to enclose Grovely Wood, which stands on the hill above the village, to create a park, but the villagers mounted a legal challenge to assert their right to cut and gather wood, which they won. They continue to exercise their rights each May, decorating the church with, in particular, fresh greenery.

If you stop by for the festival, which features many activities in addition to the cutting down of trees, make sure you take a look at the local church, too. Set into the wall surrounding it are plaques which record the price of bread over the past 150 years.

*Number of people needed to arrange a 10% group discount for visits 11
to Stonehenge*

Chris wondered what would have happened had Richard Branson been around at the time of construction...

WHAT'S WRONG WITH THIS PICTURE?

Over the centuries, Stonehenge has been drawn, painted and photographed by many great names from the art world, with varying degrees of accuracy. In general, the monument's shape and formation mean it is easily recognised, however crude the representation. But the very first depiction of the henge is easily overlooked because it shows a rectangular formation of stones.

The illustration is in a manuscript from the fourteenth century that shows a rectangular structure made up of even pillars and lintels of uniform dimensions. Fortunately the words *Stonhenges nixta Ambsebury in anglia sita* are written across the centre or it would probably have been overlooked for ever! The manuscript was intended as a history of the world and is laid out like a spreadsheet, with a line for each year, which means the illustration has been wedged into a small gap, perhaps explaining its shape. Or possibly, like early drawings of marvellous creatures such as elephants and giraffes, the image was scratched by a monk who had never actually seen the standing stones himself, and had become a trifle confused by accounts of the arrangement.

When you look at Stonehenge today you're looking at a ruin from which at least half of the original stones have been removed. Only fragments of the original, enclosing 'wall' of large Sarsen uprights with close-fitting lintels linking them remain. Of the stones that remain, many are fallen and broken, or lost beneath the turf; those that are still upright are heavily weathered. The surrounding ditch has silted up in places, and the raised bank – formed from the chalk dug out to make the ditch – worn down, so they no longer form a mighty barrier closing off the gently sloping circle in the middle of which sit the stones. In some places there is less than three feet difference between the top of the bank and bottom of the ditch.

An observer walking around the monument can be forgiven for being a little underwhelmed as they peer through the fence. However, if you can get inside the stones, or view them from above, the overall scheme – and hugeness of the undertaking – becomes more apparent. From the air you can appreciate the alignment of the monument more easily, along a north-east to south-west axis.

Within the enormous outer earthwork and ditch, with its close-by ring of concrete markers where the Aubrey Holes were once dug and timber markers may have stood, there are also two Sarsen stone blocks known as the Station Stones, which sit near the ditch to the north-west and south-east, each encircled by their own little ring ditches. From another pair of ditches that remain, it appears there was once a matching pair of stones positioned at north and south.

On the north-east to south-west axis the encircling bank breaks, forming a gap about 35 feet wide from which a causeway extends. To the east of the causeway is the 21 x 7-foot Slaughter Stone with its worn channels, once assumed to be used to drain blood, and now flat to the ground, although it may not always have been so. The final Stonehenge Sarsen stone, the Heel Stone, lies 85 feet beyond the bank.

At the centre of the enclosure created by the ditch sits what remains of the outer circle of Sarsen uprights, about 100 feet across. These in turn enclose a ring of much smaller bluestones, set about 12 feet in, most of which are little higher than a tall man. Nowadays, only six of them are still upright and many are broken, but originally there would have been around 60 or so.

Then there is an inner horseshoe of trilithons, pairs of large Sarsen uprights with a third stone across the top, with a corresponding inner horseshoe of bluestones, like the outer ring. Finally, at the centre, is the controversial Altar Stone, which probably once stood upright but has since fallen and been driven into the ground by the heavy parts of a fallen trilithon that lies on top of it.

STONEHENGE WAS BUILT BY...

Aliens

UFOlogists (as students of the UFO phenomenon are known) are renowned for their eagerness to jump onto bandwagons, so it comes as no surprise that a handful of minor theorists have suggested that Stonehenge was, in fact, the work of aliens. Some hypothesise that the trilithons were originally designed as inter-dimensional gateways (for anorexic extraterrestrials, presumably, given their narrow openings), while others believe the entire structure was intended as a spaceport. Outlandish theories of this particular sort are most popular among the followers of Erich von Däniken, whose series of bestselling 1970s pseudo-archaeological works such as *Chariots of the Gods* were predicated on the dubious idea that ancient man was far too primitive to build anything of lasting worth without outside help.

QUOTE UNQUOTE

Now to a person really capable of feeling the poetry of Stonehenge it is almost a secondary matter whether he sees Stonehenge at all...
But it does spoil his mood to find Stonehenge surrounded by a brand-new fence of barbed wire, with a policeman and a little shop selling picture post-cards.
GK Chesterton, author, writing in *A Miscellany of Men*

BEST STONEHENGE ART

The Romantics loved Stonehenge. If ever there was a vista that suggested awful majesty, it was the stones battered by storms, casting weird shadows across the heath, or standing against sunrise or sunset. Many visitors at the time were overcome by the sublime nature of the monument, so it should not be a surprise that the most dramatic paintings of the monument come from this period.

1.   JM Turner, *Stonehenge at Daybreak*, 1816
2.   JW Inchbold, *Stonehenge Sunset*, 1870s
3.   John Constable, *Stonehenge*, 1836
4.   David Logan, *Stonehenge*, seventeenth century
5.   William Blake, *The Serpent Temple*, 1818
6.   Thomas Girton, *Stonehenge with a Stormy Sky*, 1794
7.   JM Turner, *Stonehenge with Shepherd*, 1826
8.   Thomas Cole, *Stonehenge in Arcadia*, 1836
9.   John Constable, *Stonehenge*, 1832 (now lost)
10. James Bridges, *Stonehenge with Full Moon*, nineteenth century

12 ARTHURIAN ZODIAC FIGURES

The Glastonbury Zodiac is a series of giant figures that are supposedly marked out by various landmarks, ley lines, earthworks and monuments in and around Glastonbury, including Stonehenge. The discovery by Katherine Maltwood, who died in 1961, put a particularly British spin on the Zodiac, representing the 12 signs as figures in the Arthurian legends sitting around the famous Round Table, and drawing a map to show them scattered across a 10-mile circle which, believers claim, can be accurately matched up with star maps of the stellar zodiac.

Aquarius	Sir Percival, who accompanied Galahad on the Grail Quest
Leo	Lancelot, the young sun, opposite Arthur, the aged, wise sun king in the circle
Sagittarius	King Arthur, here an aged and sage king in winter
Scorpio	Mordred or Callixtus the hermit
Libra	The dove which flies through the Grail Castle leading Galahad to the Grail
Capricorn	The King of Castel Mortal, who fights with the Fisher King in the Grail legend, or Merlin
Virgo	Guinevere, leaning towards Lancelot
Gemini	Lohot, Arthur's son
Cancer	King Solomon's ship, which took Percival and Galahad to the Grail
Taurus	Sir Ector (or Hector), Arthur's foster father
Aries	Gawain, the impetuous young knight who found the Grail Castle but failed to win the prize
Pisces	The serpent-headed whale slain by Sir Percival

THE FIRST RECORD OF STONEHENGE

According to the twelfth-century chronicler Henry of Huntingdon, Stonehenge was one of four 'very remarkable' sights in England – the others were Wookey Hole, the winds of the Peak District and the heavy rainfall on some of the country's plains, highlighting something of a discrepancy between what we in the twenty-first century would regard as remarkable, and what excited the twelfth-century imagination. In *The Chronicle of Henry of Huntingdon* he wrote: 'At Stonehenge... stones of extraordinary dimensions are raised as columns, and others are fixed above, like lintels of immense portals; and no one has been able to discover by which mechanism such vast masses of stone were elevated, nor for what purpose they were designed.' Henry was an Archdeacon at Lincoln, and had been commissioned by the new Norman Bishop, Alexander of Blois, to write a history of England.

STONEHENGE AS A CALENDAR

Throughout history, humans' tendency to worship heavenly bodies as well as observe them has given calendar making a religious significance... The names of our (Western-world) months enshrine the Roman gods Janus ("January") and Mars ("March"), and the goddesses Maia ("May") and Juno ("June"). The days of our week commemorate the Teutonic and Roman deities Tiw (god of law; "Tuesday"), Woden (principal Teutonic god; "Wednesday"), Thor (god of war; "Thursday"), Fria (goddess of love; "Friday"), Saturn (god of agriculture; "Saturday"), and the sacred Sun and Moon (Sunday is "Sun's day;" Monday is "Moon's day"). The combination of religion and time-reckoning among primitive peoples achieved its most impressive expression in the megalithic ("big stone") cult of northwestern Europe (in the regions of England, Brittany, and Scandinavia). Herdsmen and farmers erected the stone structures in the centuries after 2,000 BC, that were places of worship and time-reckoning of the seasons; the largest of these is Stonehenge in southern England, Salisbury Plain, Wiltshire.

Jon E Roeckelein, *The Concept of Time in Psychology: A Resource Book and Annotated Bibliography,* 2000

CLASH OF THE CARHENGES

Back in the 1980s the Americans could boast several replica Stonehenges, including not one, but two, made from cars. During the middle of the decade, sculptor Bill Lishman was busily having cars crushed to match the size and dimensions of the original Stonehenge, before carefully erecting them in Whitby, Ontario. He christened his version 'Autohenge'. Just one year later, the papers were full of stories about 'Carhenge', a similar replica in Nebraska.

Carhenge was the brainchild of a retired engineer, James Reinders. When his father left him a farm just outside of Alliance, Nebraska, Reinders decided to create a monument out of 33 cars from the 1960s and 1970s. Gathering his family to help, he painted all of the cars battleship grey and, at a cost of US$16,000, erected them as a copy of Stonehenge, bumper down, with other vehicles precariously balanced on top to represent the lintels.

Some of Alliance's 9,000 or so inhabitants welcomed their new monument, as it brought several thousand extra visitors to the town in the first year, but others thought it was an eyesore. Despite being vandalised many times, and sprayed with graffiti, the 'ayes' eventually won out and on 19 November 1989 a new road was opened which linked the automotive henge to Highway 385.

THE MUSIC OF THE STONES

Only a handful of musicians have been inspired to call themselves Stonehenge – American Rick Nashe and the Stonehenge Band, and a bunch of Hungarian Progmeisters being the only ones that spring to mind – but many have named albums after the standing stones.

1. *Hail to the Stonehenge Gods: Tribute to Black Sabbath*, Various
2. *American Stonehenge*, Robin Williamson & His Merry Band
3. *Stonehenge: Mystic Circle*, Various
4. *Stonehenge*, Bill Russo & Richard Peaslee
5. *Stonehenge*, Runestone
6. *Stonehenge*, Ten Years After
7. *Stonehenge*, Mark Brain
8. *Sound of Mystery: Stonehenge Vols 1 & 2*, Various
9. *Stonehenge Collection*, Hawkwind
10. *Trip to Stonehenge Colony*, Cowboys & Aliens
11. *Stonehenge*, Time Machine
12. *No Sleep After Stonehenge*, David Bacha Band

QUOTE UNQUOTE

[T]he work of Stonehenge must have been that of a great and powerful nation, not of a limited community of priests.
William Borlase, English antiquary and naturalist

LEGENDARY BUILDERS

Joseph of Arimathea

There are numerous legends connecting Joseph of Arimathea with nearby Glastonbury, where he was supposed to have founded the first church in Britain, just 30 years after the death of Christ. Some recount how he brought the infant Jesus there on a merchant voyage while trading for lead! An ancient tree on Wearyall Hill, just below Glastonbury Tor, is supposed to have sprouted where Joseph planted his staff in the ground, and the Holy Grail – the chalice from the Last Supper in which Joseph is supposed to have collected Christ's blood on the cross – is rumoured to be buried there.

The Grail appears in the Glastonbury Zodiac and a few hardy souls maintain that the 'sacred architecture' of Glastonbury Abbey is echoed in the proportions of Stonehenge, and suggest that they were all built by Joseph and his followers in the first century AD. Some also maintain that Stonehenge is the resting place for the Grail, rather than any of the Glastonbury sites.

The Rollright Stones, Oxfordshire

Deep in the Cotswolds, five miles north-west of Chipping Norton, sit the four-centuries-old Rollright Stones – mere babes in terms of the age of many stone circles and monuments erected by Bronze Age and Neolithic man.

The name Rollright is thought to come from Hrolla-landright, the Land of Hrolla, rather than from the method used to move the stones into place. It's fitting, though, because the circle is one of the most perfectly formed in England, 104 feet across, sitting on the edge of a ridge that falls steeply down to the village of Long Compton. Along the edge of the ridge runs a prehistoric track, the Jurassic Way, so the stones were clearly positioned to be seen and visited easily by the builders.

Out of an estimated 105, only 77 stones remain; they would have stood originally in a close-set formation. The stones are of local oolitic limestone, which pocks and dimples spectacularly as the weather erodes it.

Like Stonehenge, the number of stones has often led to debate, especially because drawings from the 1880s depict only 25! The owners, apparently, had removed quite a few, but after the Ancient Monuments Protection Act was passed in 1882, they reinstated the majority, although quite how accurate they were in replacing them is anyone's guess.

As well as the stone circle, known locally as The King's Men, there is also a group of standing stones about 380 metres away, known as The Whispering Knights, and a single menhir, called The King's Stone, 50 metres across the road and actually in Warwickshire.

The King's Men

Often called the third great stone circle in England – after Stonehenge and Avebury, both in nearby Wiltshire – The King's Men have a colourful past, and many legends have become linked to them. The stones are supposed to be the petrified remains of a ruler and his (admittedly quite small) army who angered a local witch and were repaid by being frozen for ever.

The Whispering Knights

Five large menhirs stand adjacent to the circle and are called The Whispering Knights. They are supposed to be knights who plotted against their ruler, were caught leaning in towards each other and turned to stone. In fact, they are markers over a burial chamber about 5,000 years old, thought to be part of a long barrow and probably pre-date the circle.

The King's Stone

This may be contemporary with the stone circle. Its odd shape – some describe it as like a seal balancing a ball on its nose – has been traced to the habit local drovers had of chipping off bits that were accessible to use as charms against the Devil. Long Compton itself was, according to legend, a hotbed of witchcraft.

AN ANCIENT OBSERVATORY?

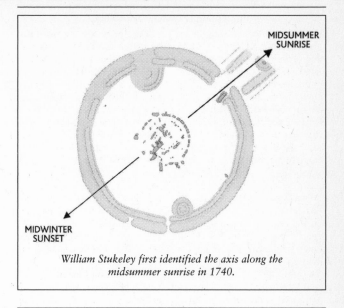

MIDSUMMER
SUNRISE

MIDWINTER
SUNSET

*William Stukeley first identified the axis along the
midsummer sunrise in 1740.*

NO GO

**Things visitors to the centre of the stone circle at Stonehenge for the
summer solstice are asked not to do:**

- Climb on the stones
- Light fires
- Bring dogs
- Play amplified music
- Put up tents
- Set off fireworks

DOWN BUT NOT OUT

Le Grand Menhir Brisé or Great Broken Menhir, is the tallest
Neolithic construction yet discovered. Although at present it is
broken into four pieces, when it was originally erected it would
have stood around 20 metres tall, and weighed around 330 tons,
which would make it the heaviest single object ever moved by man
without the help of electricity and power tools. Its remains can be
found at Locmariaquer, in Brittany, France.

LIST OF PARTS

Trilithon – term coined by William Stukeley, meaning 'three stones', from the Greek, to describe the freestanding 'gates' of stone at the centre of the Stonehenge circle.

Bluestones – smaller uprights, some rough hewn, some carefully shaped, named for their approximate colour. Many think they're greener rather than blue, and they have been found by petrologists to be made from at least five distinct types of stone.

Lintel – the large flat Sarsen stones that cap the outer ring of Sarsen stones and the trilithons.

Sarsens – the largest stones, both uprights and lintels, so called because of the particular stone they're made from.

QUOTE UNQUOTE

For many people the great monuments of Stonehenge and Avebury, with the barrows and other satellites clustering round them, represent the essential core of all British antiquity.
Historian Jacquetta Hawkes, writing in *Prehistoric Britain*

CONCRETE STONEHENGE

It was in Tudor times that scholars first began speculating as to what Stonehenge was made of. That the rock that composed most of it was alien to the landscape was apparent to them. In fact, some thought it was completely alien. John Rastell declared the stones so hard that 'no yrn tole wyll cut them without great bysynes' and decided that no one was able to quarry stones that 'be so herd so equall of bygnes and fassyon'. If they were so out of place they must have been created specially. Looking around, some theorists fixed on the great pillars of nearby Salisbury Cathedral and decided these had been formed of some supernaturally hard stuff, too, rather than the Chilmark limestone of which they were composed. By 1700 James Brome, in his *Travels over England,* was confidently telling readers that 'they are not Natural, or had their first growth here, but were Artificially cemented into that hard and durable Substance from some large Congeries of Sand...'

In other words, as the seventeenth century turned into the eighteenth century, many believed Stonehenge had been modelled out of concrete!

SLUMBERING AMONG THE STONES

Stonehenge has given you at your advanced years just such a feeling as he gave me when in my 23rd year, I passed a couple of days rambling about Salisbury Plain, the solitude and solemnities of which prompted me to write a Poem of some length in the Spenserian Stanza. I have it still in Mss and parts may be perhaps be thought worth publishing after my death among the 'juvenilia'. Overcome with heat and fatigue I took my Siesta among the Pillars of Stonehenge; but was not visited by the Muse in my Slumbers. I am therefore half tempted to think that Milton was a little of a Fibber, when he talks of his nightly visitations or when the sun purples the east.

William Wordsworth, Letter to John Kenyon, Summer 1838

BUYING STONEHENGE

Until comparatively recently, Stonehenge has been in private hands – often hands that were ill-disposed to lay out the large sums of money needed to ensure stones didn't fall down or were made safe for onlookers. It wasn't until 1913 that an act was passed to make sure important privately owned monuments such as Stonehenge couldn't be pulled down or summarily sold and transported to other countries.

Stonehenge came up for sale by auction on 21 September 1915, when the last private owner, Sir Edmund Antrobus, died in active service in World War I. The last attempt to buy the monument to preserve it had been made a few years earlier, when American philanthropist John Jacob Astor tried to buy it from Sir Edmund for £25,000, intending to gift it to the British Museum. Perhaps because of the economic downturn caused by the war, when it actually went under the hammer it sold for just £6,600, and was purchased by Mr Cecil Chubb, a local landowner. Although colourful stories circulate to this day that he bought it on a whim as a birthday present for his wife, reports at the time suggested he merely thought it should really be owned by a local man.

For three years Chubb ran the monument, allowing visitors in for a reasonable sum which nonetheless provided a good return on his investment, letting people carry out their rituals without interference, but by 1918, he seemed to have grown tired of his stewardship, and made a gift of it to the nation, collecting a knighthood in the process. Afterwards, the locals liked to call him Viscount Chubb of Stonehenge.

Braemore House

You have to dip into Hampshire for a few miles to reach Braemore House, north of Fordingbridge, but it's worth it if you want to try your luck navigating the compact maze – known as the Mizmaze – in its grounds. The house itself is a lavish Elizabethan manor, built by the Doddington family in the 1580s, then partly rebuilt in the mid-nineteenth century after a fire.

Inside is the usual country house mishmash of good and indifferent paintings (including, bizarrely, a series from Mexico), tapestries, furniture and a rare James I carpet. Pevsner, in his *Buildings of England*, noted that the front was 'plain and sensible' and the dining room possessed of a chimney piece which has 'two strapping girls, placed left and right, and in the overmantle a fine cartouche'. The more mature petrolhead will enjoy pottering around the tractors and steam engines on display in the Braemore Countryside Museum which is nearby, while everyone else can enjoy a cream tea or stroll around the village enjoying the thatched cottages and village green, imagining themselves in the pages of an Agatha Christie novel.

QUICK CUT

In 2003, new laser scanning techniques were used on areas of three of the monoliths at Stonehenge, and were able to detect images that were just a few millimetres deep, which have been badly eroded in places. The pictures are supposed to be of Bronze axe heads, like those found in barrows nearby. Similar images have been found engraved on rocks at Bronze Age burial sites across the UK. Wessex Archaeology and Archaeoptics, the companies that carried out the scan, are reported to regard this as evidence that Stonehenge was used as a funeral monument, even if it may not have been built as one originally.

The earliest record of carvings being spotted on the stones dates from 1953 and the images appear to have worn a great deal in the 50 years since they were first photographed. Due to the fact that Bronze axe heads were not used until at least 500 years after the final phase of construction at Stonehenge, the carvings may, in fact, be signs of a secondary use for the structure.

The axe head images were found after just 30 minutes of scanning. The scanning was concentrated on places where images had previously been seen and only aimed at small areas of the monoliths.

STONEHENGE FROM THE AIR

There are many wonderful photographs available now of Stonehenge from the air, and most people agree that it's much easier to understand the layout of the stones and the surrounding topography while looking at aerial shots. The earliest surviving aerial photograph of Stonehenge was taken from a military balloon in 1906, but until 1933, most investigators didn't have the luxury of consulting a consistent series of aerial photographs of the area. Major GW Allen, a pioneering aerial surveyor, began making several passes over the ancient monument. Fourteen of the surviving photos he took, from 1933 to 1936, showed clear structures like the avenue and cursus (a long, narrow, rectangular earthwork enclosure), and the surrounding barrows, and are now held as part of a larger archive of his work at the Antiquities Department at the Ashmolean Museum, Oxford.

VISITOR NUMBERS TO STONEHENGE IN RECENT YEARS

1997/1998	775,835
1998/1999	832,540
1999/2000	836,294
2000/2001	790,427
2001/2002	713,565
2002/2003	755,744
2003/2004	757,721

(Source: English Heritage)

STONEHENGE FAIR

Stonehenge used to be the site of a thriving fair. In 1680 (or 1690 according to some sources), Thomas Hayward obtained a Royal Warrant – which is still in power today – to hold an autumn fair at Stonehenge on 25-26 September. The fair grew into a large gathering, important in the area, and was later moved to the summer solstice. Some archaeologists believe some of the inexplicable holes detected on the site may have been places that sellers dug out to support posts holding up their stalls.

Perhaps the most outlandish theory associated with Stonehenge is the idea that the Olympic Games are derived from games held at the Cursus in ancient times. Pindar is sometimes given as a source for this notion, and supporters note that the local people would assemble at Stonehenge to play games into the nineteenth century. On 1 July, Victorian village cricketers and football players would assemble near the stones and hold a tournament.

INTRICATE PROFUSION

Three summer days I roamed, when 'twas my chance
To have before me on the downy plain
Lines, circles, mounds, a mystery of shapes
Such as in many quarters yet survive,
With intricate profusion figuring o'er
The untilled ground (the work, as some divine,
Of infant science, imitative forms
By which the Druids covertly expressed
Their knowledge of the heavens, and imaged forth
The constellations), I was gently charmed
Albeit with an antiquarian's dream,
And saw the bearded teachers, with white wands
Uplifted, pointing to the starry sky,
Alternately, and plain below, while breath
Of music seemed to guide them, and the waste
Was cheared with stillness and a pleasant sound.

William Wordsworth, from *The Prelude*

CASTING THE RUNES

According to legend, Stonehenge might have been built as a
monument to which English ruler?
a) King Canute
b) Alfred the Great
c) King Arthur
d) Hengist
Answer on page 153.

NUMBERING THE STONES

The convention when describing Stonehenge is to follow a numbering
system created by William Flinders Petrie, which begins with the
outer Sarsen uprights (numbers 1-30) and continues to include all the
stones that are thought to have made up the monument before any
were removed. The outer ring of bluestones are numbered 31-49,
with added letters for broken stones, plus stone 150, a bluestone that
was once intended as a lintel but was reused for this ring. The inner
trilithon uprights are numbers 51-60, and their lintels 152, 154, 156,
158 and 160. The lintels on the outer circle, a little confusingly,
number 101-130, while the inner horseshoe of bluestones account for
numbers 61-72. Of the odd stones, the Altar Stone is numbered 80,
and the four Station Stones are 91-94.

STONEHENGE WAS BUILT BY...

The French

In the late 1990s, following the discovery of faint carvings on one of the stones, Aubrey Burl suggested Stonehenge had been built by the French. Or more properly by Celts from Brittany. He based this on the similarity in carvings, and the likeness between Stonehenge's design and that of 16 older Breton megalithic sites. He pointed out many Breton sites have a horseshoe formation, similar to that of the central trilithons of Stonehenge, and that while other British Neolithic structures don't have corner stones like those at Stonehenge, there is one at Crucuno in Brittany that shares this feature. Burl also noticed similarities between a newly discovered box-like form, which he traces back to scratched depictions of a female guardian of the dead found on French examples.

Others have since suggested that the migratory tribes which came into Wessex had previously made contact with people in Brittany and picked up some design ideas from them. The main problem with this theory is that historians have dated the 'similar' Breton temples as being 1,000 years older than Stonehenge, and while they do share a horseshoe ground plan, there are no trilithons constructed in Brittany.

QUOTE UNQUOTE

As prodigious as any tales I ever heard of them and worth going this journey to see. God knows what their use was!
Samuel Pepys, diarist

VIEWS OF STONEHENGE

If you compare early paintings and drawings of Stonehenge to the modern landscape, you'll see that although the stones have changed very little themselves, what surrounds them has altered quite a bit. Up until the late eighteenth century they sat in open downland, used to graze sheep in the summer and largely abandoned in the winter.

All this was changed by the 3rd Duke of Queensbury, who had carefully arranged plantings of trees put in to improve the views around Amesbury.

Further forestation took place in the nineteenth century. The areas known as Fargo Plantation and Normanton Gorse were added at this period, and trees were still being planted north of Stonehenge, sometimes over Neolithic sites, into the twentieth century. The trend has now been reversed, and trees that are at risk of damaging important sites are being cut down. But of course we, with our motorways and slip roads, can never reclaim the original views enjoyed by our ancestors.

BEST FILMS FEATURING STONEHENGE

1. *This is Spinal Tap* (1984)
The funniest, and quite possibly most accurate, film ever made about rock music.

2. *Mars Attacks!* (1996)
Stonehenge gets bowled over by the invading Martians.

3. *Tess* (1979)
Roman Polanski was in danger of being extradited to America if he set foot in England, so Stonehenge had to be recreated in plastic and set up in Brittany for the film.

4. *Help!* (1965)
Richard Lester's glorious romp starring the Beatles, in which the police decide the ideal place to 'hide' the Fab Four is in the middle of Salisbury Plain.

5. *Night of the Demon* (1957)
Dennis Wheatley knock-off in which a paranormal psychologist falls foul of an evil cult who want to sacrifice him to a demon. Hokey fun.

6. *Still Crazy* (1998)
A warm-hearted Clements/La Frenais feature film about a bunch of ageing musicians who are spurred on to regroup when one of their number dies. After gathering in Avebury they have a few beers and go strolling among the stones. OK, it's not Stonehenge, but it is quite a good film with Timothy Spall and Bill Nighy.

7. *King Lear* (1983)
Laurence Olivier's last crack at Shakespeare on film, which symbolically begins and ends at Stonehenge.

8. *The Small Back Room* (1949)
A lesser-known Powell and Pressburger film that relies a great deal on landscape and ambience to get its message across. At the beginning the hero visits Stonehenge to test a new weapon, which is shot close up as a towering and almost claustrophobic presence.

GUIDANCE FROM GEORGIA

Unlike the many copies of Stonehenge that have been built in America in the last century or so, the Georgia Guidestones near Nuberg consist of just six large slabs erected on a hilltop. The 19-foot chunks of granite were put there by RC Christian, a man about whom very little is known, around 1980, and were apparently funded by a small group of ethically-minded private citizens.

The stones are inscribed with 10 laws which aim to 'unite humanity', repeated in 12 languages. The edicts have a decidedly modern tone, unlike the original 10 Commandments, and include 'avoid useless officials' and 'guide reproduction wisely'.

OTHER NAMES FOR THE SUMMER SOLSTICE...

...or the night before, and who celebrates it

Vestalia .... Romans
Feast of Epona .... Gauls
Alben Heruin .... Druids
Ukon juhla .... Ancient Finns
Juhannus .... Modern Finns
Feast of St John the Baptist .... Christians
Sonnwend .... Germans
Bonfire Night .... Irish
Ivan Kupala Day .... Russians and the Ukrainians
Kupole .... Lithuanians
Sankthansaften or Jonsok .... Norwegians
Midsommar .... Swedes
Sankt Hans aften .... Danes
Feill-Sheathain .... Celts
Litha .... Saxons and Neo Pagans
Johannistag or Sommerweihnacht ... Germanic and Baltic Christians
Jani .... Latvians
Thing-Tide .... Norsemen
Noc wwittojasska .... Polish

VICTORIAN STONEHENGE

Victorian visitors to Stonehenge would be greeted by one of the monument's string of eccentric guardians: first, Henry Browne, proponent of Catastrophism and zealous lecturer, then his son Joseph, followed by William Judd, who introduced a mobile photographic studio to the stones, and finally, towards the close of the century, by 'Sikher' Smeeth, a former soldier in the Indian Army. Although these guardians received often lavish tips for their services guiding visitors, they were not allowed to sell refreshments, so guidebooks of the time always advised taking a well-stocked hamper with you.

In 1857, access to the stones was opened up by the arrival of a train line from London to Salisbury, making day trips possible. Enterprising locals put on horse-drawn carts from the station which cost five shillings – a not inconsiderable sum at the time. Stonehenge became a common social destination for local groups, too. Cricket matches and other sporting contests were often held there in summer, hunts and coursers met there, and it became a venue for annual Sunday School and club outings. There is even record of a theatrical troupe, the Magpie Musicians, putting on a concert in 1896.

MASTER BUILDERS

The list of people who are supposed to have built Stonehenge goes on and on – from the prehistoric to the positively futuristic:

Neolithic Brits • Bronze Age Brits

Druids • Merlin

Egyptians • Giants

Danes • Romans

Celts • Greeks

Phoenicians • Welsh

Saxons • Atlanteans

Aliens • French

A SOLEMN, AWFUL PLACE

Friday, 27 August 1875

To-day I paid my first visit to Stonehenge. We had breakfast before Church and immediately after service Morris and I started to walk to Stonehenge, eleven miles. Passing through the beautiful Cathedral Close and, the city of Salisbury we took the Devizes road and after we had walked along that road for some six miles we saw in the dim distance the mysterious Stones standing upon the Plain. The sun was hot, but a sweet soft air moved over the Plain 'wafting' the scent of the purple heather tufts and the beds of thyme and making the delicate blue harebells tremble on their fragile stems. A beautiful little wheatear flitted before us from one stone heap to another along the side of the wheel track as we struck across the firm elastic turf. Around us the Plain heaved mournfully with great and solemn barrows, the 'grassy barrows of the happier dead'.

Soon after we left the Druid's Head and struck across the turf eastward we came in sight of the grey cluster of gigantic Stones. They stood in the midst of a green plain, and the first impression they left on my mind was that of a group of people standing about and talking together. It seemed to me as if they were ancient giants who suddenly became silent and stiffened into stone, directly anyone approached, but who might at any moment become alive again, and at certain seasons, as at midnight and on Old Christmas and Midsummers Eve, might form a true 'Chorea Gigantum' and circle on the Plain in a solemn and stately dance. It is a solemn awful place. As I entered the charmed circle of the sombre Stones I instinctively uncovered my head. It was like entering a great Cathedral Church.

Robert Francis Kilvert, *Kilvert's Diary 1870-1879*

28 *Year in the twentieth century in which William Hawley finished his survey of Stonehenge*

AN A-Z OF WORLD HERITAGE SITES

(and the date of their first listing)

Australia	Great Barrier Reef (1981)
Belgium	La Grand-Place, Brussels (1998)
Cambodia	Angkor (1992)
Denmark	Roskilde Cathedral (1995)
Egypt	Ancient Thebes with its Necropolis (1979)
England	Stonehenge (1986)
France	Mont-Saint-Michel and its Bay (1979)
Greece	Archaeological Site of Delphi (1987)
Honduras	Maya Site of Copan (1980)
India	Taj Mahal (1983)
Jordan	Petra (1985)
Kenya	Mount Kenya National Park/Natural Forest (1997)
Lebanon	Tyre (1984)
Mali	Timbuktu (1988)
Nepal	Kathmandu Valley (1979)
Oman	Archaeological Sites of Bat, Al-Khutm and Al-Ayn (1988)
Peru	Historic Sanctuary of Machu Picchu (1983)
Spain	Alhambra, Generalife, Albayzin, Granada (1984)
Tunisia	Site of Carthage (1979)
USA	Yellowstone National Park (1978)
Vietnam	Ha Long Bay (1994)
Yemen	Old Walled City of Shibam (1982)
Zimbabwe	Mosi-oa-Tunya/Victoria Falls (1989)

QUOTE UNQUOTE

*The misfortune of ruins – to be beheld nearly always at
noonday by visitors, and not at twilight.*
Thomas Hardy, author, following a visit to Stonehenge

SPOOKY STONEHENGE

A hum-dinger!
Throughout history people have reported hearing strange sounds while visiting Stonehenge, and indeed auditory phenomena are particularly associated with crop circles with which the area is also identified. In one of the more famous modern 'events', visitors reported hearing an odd buzzing emanating from the direction of the stones. As they approached they described the noise as going up into the sky. Looking up, they caught sight of a wheel of fire turning as it ascended into the heavens from which the sound seemed to come.

Number of stones in one of the two rings thought to mark the days of 29
the lunar month

'A Week at Land's End', JT Blight, 1856

CASTING THE RUNES

Approximately how many stone circles are there still
at least partially standing in the British Isles?
a) 250-300
b) 600-650
c) 900-950
d) 2,500-2,600
Answer on page 153.

PRE-STONEHENGE PITS

During work on an extension to the visitor's car park four (or possibly
five) large postholes were found, all dating from the Mesolithic period
before construction on Stonehenge began. The dubious fifth hole may
have been where the root of a large tree once sat. In 8,000 BC, the holes
held pine posts nearly two and a half feet thick, which rotted *in situ*, and
three of them seem to have been aligned on a rough east-west axis.
Nothing similar has ever been found in Britain that dates so far back,
but rows of posts from a similar period have been found in Scandinavia.

THE STONEHENGE FREE FESTIVAL

In late June, many of the visitors to Stonehenge are youngsters who have stopped off on their way to or from the Glastonbury Music Festival which – while massive and, to many old-timers, so woefully commercial – still nonetheless remains the most laid-back major festival on offer to any would-be free spirits (when it is being held). You may have to pay more than £100 for three days of music, but at least you still get to share cold taps and malodorous toilets with thousands of other ravers, giving it that true festival feel.

However, from 1972 to 1985, those in search of liberty and nature never got as far as Glastonbury. Instead, they made their way to the Stonehenge Free Festival. Originally started (following police interference which shut down the Windsor Free Festival) as a celebration of midsummer, the festival attracted an eclectic mix of maturing hippies, potheads, peaceniks and activists who, in the early years, gathered in a field next to the monument and proceeded to play loud music and consume prolific amounts of illegal substances, doing little harm to anyone.

At first the festival attracted small numbers, and was peaceful and relaxed, a place where all kinds of people could mix. But like so many events, it became a victim of its own success.

Increased numbers meant more problems with traffic, rubbish and the local population. By 1984, the last time the festival was held, 30,000 free thinkers, New Age travellers and music lovers gathered. Unfortunately, they were also joined by a significant number of criminals.

It all came to an end in 1985 at the 'Battle of the Beanfield', when police forced a large convoy of New Age travellers headed for the festival off the road and arrested over 500 of them. Many were able to escape into nearby woods, but the festival itself was halted.

The group had first formed at Greenham Common in 1982, and in summer 1986 the police, magistrates and local landowners continued to force the travellers off sites and split them up into smaller groups. Vehicles were confiscated, children were taken into care, and adults arrested again, as local farmers blocked routes and attempted to turn the convoy back.

In 1987, English Heritage tried a peaceful compromise by setting up a ticket-only festival, with 500 places on offer, and giving those gathered at the site access to the stones. But a number of would-be attendees decided, instead, to visit the Glastonbury Festival and the experiment was quietly dropped.

THE DRUID PANTHEON

Druids worship a huge variety of spirits, gods and goddesses whose links to pre-Celtic religions are sometimes a little vague. Their literature provides a god for mostly every occasion such as Arganto-rota, the goddess of Astronomic Cyclicality (whatever that may be) and Dewa, the goddess of Fluvial Moisture. Just in case you need to know where to direct your prayers, here's a few suggestions...

Adabandinos	god of music
Ambaxtonos	god of agriculture
Agrona	goddess of carnage
Aidu-manda	goddess of sunburn
Buccos	god of male vitality
Cucciraeta	goddess of boating
Danua	god of abundance
Liros	god of the tides
Lugos	god of oaths
Lutanios	god of carpenters
Matrona	goddess of maternity
Rigatona (easily mistaken for a pasta shape)	goddess of sovereignty
Vaea	goddess of hatred
Viridios	the Green Man

QUOTE UNQUOTE

Giants and Woden (alias Grim) were credited with the building of earthworks and megalithic monuments by the Anglo-Saxons, and that both were often replaced in medieval times by the Devil. Indeed, the Bath architect John Wood, writing in 1747, gives a story in which the Devil, not Merlin, transports Stonehenge to Salisbury Plain.
Jennifer Westwood, author

IN THE WORLD OF THE DEAD ALBION

And the great voice of the Atlantic howled over the Druid altars,
Weeping over his children in Stonehenge, in Maldon and Colchester,
Round the rocky Peak of Derbyshire, London Stone and
Rosamond's bower:
'What is a wife and what is a harlot? What is a church and what
Is a theatre? Are they two and not one? Can they exist separate?
Are not religion and politics the same thing? Brotherhood is religion;
Oh demonstrations of reason, dividing families in cruelty and pride!'
William Blake, from *Jerusalem: The Emanation of the Giant Albion*, 1820

The Nether Wallop Pyramid

Dr Francis Douce was a man who liked a bargain. When he died in 1765, he left £1,000 to endow a school in the village of Nether Wallop and to care for its old people. But this was on condition that the parish maintained his unusual grave marker – an 11-foot grey stone pyramid which originally had a red-painted carving of flames on the top. The pyramid was surrounded by iron railings, and his will instructed 'that my pyramid shall be kept in good order and the iron rails painted every second year at the charge of the parish'. But as any visitor today will notice, the iron railings are gone, and the inscription, 'Here lye the Remains of FRANCIS DOUCE Doctor of Phyfick', is barely legible.

The pyramid is in the grounds of St Andrew's church, at the end of a lane off the main road through the village, which lies off the A343 from Andover.

TORNADO MONUMENTS

Doctor Terence Meaden, a noted meteorologist who first came to popular attention for his 'plasma vortex' theory of how crop circles were created, applied his meteorological knowledge to the nature of the cursi (rectangular earthwork enclosures) created by Neolithic man, and came to the intriguing conclusion that they were monuments to the paths of ancient tornados.

According to his theory primitive man in many places worshiped the concept of an earth mother goddess and a sky father god, and the tornado, for them, was a rather obvious, phallic representation of the sky coupling with the Earth. During the 1990s he published two books, *The Stonehenge Solution* and *Stonehenge: The Secret of the Solstice*, about his hypothesis.

The sceptic will immediately say 'But we don't have tornados in England', but in fact we do... around 35 a year on average. Interestingly, tornados, at least in Britain, tend to move from west to east or sometimes south-west to north-east – a direction echoed in the orientation of many of the ancient cursi found so far. Meaden also pointed out that the tree-flattening effect of a tornado in a woody area would make the digging of the commemorative ditches much easier, and suggests that the communion between the two major gods would have been sufficient motivation to get whole populations digging. In 1979 there was a tornado reported near Stonehenge, which cut a swathe 50 metres wide through a planting of trees in Figheldean. Having mapped out the area where this divine communion took place, Neolithic man may then have regarded it as sacred and wished to bury his dead there.

SPOOKY STONEHENGE

Full moon spectres

When the moon is full, small spectral figures can allegedly be seen running among the stones that make up the great stone circle at Avebury. Witnesses have reported hearing music and seeing lights flickering, and some believe this is a ghostly imprint of Avebury Fair which, up to Victorian times, was held in the village within the stone circle. The theory is that certain events, especially those with a strong emotional content, can imprint themselves on a location and are occasionally replayed for sensitive watchers.

WHILE YOU'RE IN THE AREA WHY NOT VISIT...

The Bulford Kiwi

In an area famous for mysterious chalk carvings on the hills, modern man has also left his mark. Scattered around Salisbury Plain are numerous regimental crests carved into the hillsides, memorials to the thousands of British and Commonwealth troops who were stationed in the area during World War I. The area around Fount, Compton Chamberleyne and Sutton Manderville is particularly rich in giant badge outlines, but perhaps the most startling chalk image in the area is the giant kiwi, cut into the green slope of the hill north of Bulford.

The Bulford Kiwi is a mighty 420 feet across; the beak alone measures 150 feet. It was created in 1918 by soldiers from New Zealand – one suspects as a way of keeping themselves occupied while they waited to be shipped home. The man ordered to design the kiwi motif before the men started digging, Sergeant Major Percy Blenkarne, hadn't actually seen his national bird before, but he didn't let that hold him back. Setting out at once for the Natural History Museum in London, he arrived late at night but managed to persuade the caretaker to let him in. He found a picture of a kiwi and made a quick sketch, before returning to Wiltshire. Once back at the army camp he lost no time in pegging out what is in essence a great big blob with legs and a beak sticking out, and added a 65-foot-high NZ signature for good measure.

Once Percy Blenkarne had returned to Auckland along with the other troops, it was the Kiwi Boot Polish Company who took over maintenance of the carving, in effect a giant natural billboard for the firm's product, until 1967, when it was left to local army units to organise its upkeep. People have complained about their proficiency in doing so from time to time, without taking into account the effort needed – they need to re-lay around 20 tons of chalk every six months just to keep it looking white.

TOP RATED STONE CIRCLES IN
THE REPUBLIC OF IRELAND...

...according to www.megalithic.co.uk, whose researchers rank each site for overall condition, ambience and ease of access. Scoring is out of 15, with only the sites that achieve 10 points or more listed.

Derreenataggart, Co Cork, 14
Kilmartin Lower, Co Cork, 14
Glanbrack, Co Cork, 13
Ardgroom, Co Cork, 12
Bauraglanna, Co Tipperary, 12
Drombohilly, Co Kerry, 12
Kealkil, Co Cork, 12
Kenmare, Co Kerry, 12
Templebryan, Co Cork, 12
Uragh NE, Co Kerry, 12
Athgreany, Co Wicklow, 11
Carrowmore 11, 26 and 57, Co Sligo, 11
Cong N, Co Mayo, 11
Cowmore 9, Co Sligo, 11
Gowlane N, Co Cork, 11
Gurteen, Co Kerry, 11
Knockraheen Stone Circle, Co Cork, 11
Lough Gur C, Co Limerick, 11
Uragh SW, Co Kerry, 11
Annagannihy SE, Co Cork, 10
Cong W, Co Mayo, 10
Dunbeacon, Co Cork, 10
Glantane SW Stone Circle, Co Cork, 10
Grange, Co Limerick, 10
Inchireagh, Co Cork, 10
Kilmeedy W, Co Cork, 10
Trawlebane, Co Cork, 10

THE INNER BLUESTONE HORSESHOE

Unlike the outer ring of bluestones just within the Sarsen uprights, the bluestones that echo the form of the five trilithons towards the centre of the circle have been carefully dressed. Originally there were 19, but now only six remain – being smaller, the bluestones were more at risk from locals looking for some building stone in an area whose chief deposits are flaky chalk unsuitable for building. Each of the six bluestones has been formed into a square pillar, about two feet across and, similar to the trilithons, their heights vary. They seem to have been arranged to rise in height towards the south-west, ranging from six- to eight-feet high.

Number of disc-shaped barrows in the vicinity of Stonehenge that contain 35
signs of cremation

WRITTEN AT STONEHENGE

Thou noblest monument of Albion's isle!
Whether by Merlin's aid from Scythia's shore,
To Amber's fatal plain Pendragon bore,
Huge frame of giant-hands, the mighty pile,
T'entomb his Britons slain by Hengist's guile:
Or Druid priests, sprinkled with human gore,
Taught 'mid thy massy maze their mystic lore:
Or Danish chiefs, enrich'd with savage spoil,
To Victory's idol vast, an unhewn shrine,
Rear'd the rude heap: or, in thy hallow'd round,
Repose the kings of Brutus' genuine line;
Or here those kings in solemn state were crown'd:
Studious to trace thy wondrous origine,
We muse on many an ancient tale renown'd.

Thomas Wharton, *The Pleasures of Melancholy,*
c. 1745-1747

QUOTE UNQUOTE

Every age has the Stonehenge it deserves – or desires.
Historian Jacquetta Hawkes

THE FACE OF STONEHENGE

Although millions upon millions of people visiting Stonehenge have looked at stone 54 from every conceivable angle, it wasn't until the twenty-first century that anyone noticed that if you looked at the outer side of this particular stone, it appears to have been carved into a relief sculpture of a human face. The carving is up to 7.5 centimetres deep, and depicts a strong face with a long nose and distinguished eyebrows.

At certain times of the day it appears quite distinct, even from a distance (around 2pm to 2.30pm is the recommended time to view it in the summer, because the sunlight brings it out. If you approach the monument from the west at this time on a sunny day, the relief is visible up to 30 metres away). Much attention has been paid to the stone next to it since carvings were discovered on it around 50 years ago, but it took someone looking the right way at just the right moment to spot this phenomenon.

Similar carvings have been noted at Avebury on many of the stones, and it is theorised that they were done to face different sunrises and sunsets.

FACTS AND FIGURES

1.4 metres – average distance between Sarsen stones

2 metres – average width of the Sarsen stones

3 metres – average length of the lintels connecting them

5 tons – weight of the average bluestone

6 metres – height of the tallest Sarsen stone

17 – number of Sarsen stones still standing in the outer circle

30 – number of Sarsen stones in the outer circle

32 kilometres – the distance from the Marlborough Downs that the Sarsen stones were probably dragged

40 tons – weight of an average Sarsen upright

200 – the number of men that would have been needed to drag one of the Sarsen stones from the Marlborough Downs

240 kilometres – distance the bluestones were transported if they came from the Preseli Mountains in Wales

1,400 years – the length of time over which the monument was constructed

THE VAGINA MONOLITHS

Just when you're sure you've heard all the possible strange explanations for Stonehenge, a new one pops up out of left field. In July 2003, newspapers picked up the story of a paper published by Anthony Perks, a gynaecologist and researcher at the University of British Columbia in the *Journal of the Royal Society of Medicine*. In it he claimed that Stonehenge and other stone circles were temples to a Neolithic Earth Mother goddess built to represent her vagina. 'Stonehenge could represent the opening by which the Earth Mother gave birth to plants and animals on which ancient people so depended,' he told a reporter from *The Observer*. Within his article Perks identified differences between the two stones used in each of the trilithons, and believes that the different textures of each pair were supposed to represent male and female principals, joined together by the lintels. He also demonstrated that overhead shots of Stonehenge showed marked similarities to female genitalia.

However, Perks seems to have got some fundamental details wrong. He went on to tell reporters that there are no burials around Stonehenge – 'There is little sign of death; there are no tombs, because Stonehenge was a place of life' – and dated the whole construction to around 3,000 BC.

In an effort to refine and clarify the dates of the different phases of activity at Stonehenge, English Heritage got its Scientific Dating Service to work in tandem with Wessex Archaeology, who has a lot of specialist knowledge of the area. They called upon the services of the high-precision radiocarbon dating laboratory at Queen's University, Belfast, and the Oxford Radiocarbon Accelerator Unit, as well as other specialists, to provide the most accurate estimates to date.

As well as providing reliable dates for each major phase of construction, they hoped to clarify the sequence of events involved in the erection of the main stone circle, inner trilithons, bluestones and various marker stones, and finally be able to ascribe each stone to a specific phase through radiocarbon dating.

Their first stage was to look again at the results of previous attempts, and to re-examine the samples used. Several were rejected and new samples selected which the teams regarded as pure and, most importantly, from areas where enough similar material remained to allow future researchers to duplicate the experiment. Fifty-two reliable samples were found, and by freshly examining them and subjecting them to radiocarbon dating the team produced the following:

Multiple samples of charcoal found in large pits that once contained posts under the car park during excavations in 1966, were from pine dated between 8,500 and 6,700 BC, making them from the Mesolithic period.

Analysis of nine different samples of antlers found in the ditch forming the henge put the date of the first phase of construction at between 3,000 and 2,920 BC.

There are no useful radiocarbon dates from the next stage of Stonehenge which saw timber structures and the digging of the Aubrey Holes.

The bluestones first arrived in around 2,550 BC and were followed, a century or so later by the Sarsens. The outer circle and the inner horseshoe were raised between 2,440 and 2,100 BC, but most probably some time around 2,300 BC. This was the same date as the burial of a man who had been killed with flint arrows and was buried in the partly silted ditch.

The bluestones, which appear to have been removed for a while, reappear some time between 2,280 and 1,930 BC and were arranged in the settings that can be seen today.

38 *Diameter in metres of the wooden structure to the south-east of the Durrington Walls henge, which is near Stonehenge*

AMERICAN HENGES

10 replicas from the 50 states:

1. **Sam Hill's Stonehenge,** Maryhill, Washington
2. **Carhenge,** Alliance, Nebraska
3. **Foamhenge,** Natural Bridge, Virginia
4. **Fridgehenge,** Santa Fe, New Mexico (there was also a Fridgehenge in New Zealand, but now demolished)
5. **Stubby Stonehenge,** Rolla, Missouri
6. **Golfhenge,** Fortine, Montana
7. **Stonehenge II,** Kerrville, Texas
8. **America's Stonehenge,** North Salem, New Hampshire
9. **Subdivision Stonehenge,** Athens, Georgia
10. **Mystical Horizons,** Turtle Mountains, Cadbury, North Dakota

---

CASTING THE RUNES

What is the name of the person who discovered the Aubrey Holes?
a) John Aubrey
b) Aubrey Beardsley
c) James Aubrey
d) Alexander Aubrey Drew
Answer on page 153.

THINK PINK

The area that surrounds Carnac in the north of France is rich in Roman remains, and Scottish antiquarian James Miln investigated both Neolithic and Roman sites in the area during the 1860s and 1870s. He employed a local lad, Zacharie Le Rouzic, to help carry his equipment and inspired Le Rouzic, many years later during the 1930s, to raise many of the fallen stones. Le Rouzic worked assiduously and marked every stone he moved with a bit of pink cement on the base, so future generations would know exactly what had been altered. When Miln died in 1881, he left his work to the town of Carnac, and his brother set up a museum there which, together with artefacts donated by Le Rouzic, formed the basis of the collection which can now be seen at the Carnac Museum of Pre-History. A more detailed survey of the Carnac site wasn't undertaken until 1969. It was carried out by Alexander Thom and his son Archie. From 1970 to 1974, the two mapped the 3,000 menhirs, and discovered that some of the alignments were not as straight as had been previously thought.

Rival historians Smythe and Jennings always enjoyed their Stonehenge debates...

SUPERNATURAL STONEHENGE

I was not the only spectator. A solitary stranger was visible from time to time, who, without seeming to perceive me, had been going round and round among the stones incessantly for the last quarter of an hour. He was evidently counting, and seemed very impatient of something. The next time he emerged, I took the liberty to ask him the source of his singular demeanour; on which he politely answered, that he had been told no one could count these stones aright; that every time the number was different; and that this was a trick which Satan, the author of the work, played the curious: that he had within the last two hours confirmed the truth of this statement seven times, and that he should inevitably lose his senses if he tried again. I advised him to leave off, and go home, as it was growing dark, and Satan might play him a worse trick than this. He fixed his eyes upon me sarcastically, and with what the Scotch call a very 'uncanny' expression, looked about him as if for somebody; then suddenly explaining 'Good-bye, Sir!' strode off, like Peter Schleimil, casting no shadow (tis true the sun was set) with seven-league steps across the down, where he disappeared behind the hill.

Prince Pueckler-Muskau, upon visiting Stonehenge from Salisbury on 28 December 1832

Giant rocks moved by magic power (D2136.1) are also found in Chaucer Franklin's Tale, where the magician removes the stones from the coast of Brittany. Presumably these rocks were all moved in the twinkling of an eye, and such marvellous speed is a common occurrence in folk tradition.
Stith Thompson, folklorist, writing in *The Folktale*

BEST OF BRITISH

The Callanish Stones, Isle of Lewis

The Scottish islands provide a lot for Neolithic enthusiasts, and none more so than the Isle of Lewis. The Callanish Stones consist of several ancient monuments near the village of Callanish, close to Stornoway. The most inspiring is Callanish I, a slightly ovoid ring 13.1 x 11.3 metres, formed by 13 tall, thin stones made from the silvery gneiss common on Lewis. In the centre of the ring is a slightly taller stone. It is about 4.75 metres tall, and is reached by four avenues at the cardinal points. Those to the south, east and west are marked by a single row of standing stones, while that to the north has a double row.

Within the circle lies a round cairn that dates from somewhere in the Neolithic period, but experts are unsure whether it was built before, after or during the construction of the circle, which was around 1,800 BC. There are three other stone circles of a similar age nearby: Cnoc Ceann à Gharaidh (also known as Callanish II); Cnoc Filibhir Bheag (Callanish III); and Ceann Hulavig (Callanish IV). Callanish II consists of seven stones, two now fallen, that form a curved screen around a now-ruined cairn. Looking east-south-east of Callanish I you can see the third monument sitting on a low ridge, of which 12 stones remain standing, following the pattern of two concentric ellipses. A little further to the south is Callanish IV, where five standing stones crowd around a cairn.

In recent years, a further stone circle has been discovered on a ridge overlooking Callanish I, erected beside the quarry from which the gneiss for the entire monument was dug. Neolithic quarries are rare finds, and the new circle, called Na Dromannan, is much bigger than the more famous ones nearby, being about 30 metres across, and made up of stones approximately four metres high and 2.3 metres wide.

Local legends say the island was once a haunt of giants who, when St Kieran arrived, refused to be converted to Christianity. The saint then turned them into stones. Folklore also references the ancient rites of the Summer King, talking of a 'shining one' who walks along the stone avenue on Midsummer morning.

Salisbury

In 2005, Salisbury was voted one of the top 10 places to visit in the UK by readers of *The Observer*. While it's a good staging point for visiting the local monoliths and barrows, it's also an ancient city with many charming buildings and, of course, a famous cathedral with its 123-metre-high spire – the tallest in Britain. While you're there, try to get into the thirteenth century banqueting hall in Cathedral Close.

Mompesson House, also in Cathedral Close, is a wonderful example of Queen Anne architecture: neat, symmetrical and perfectly proportioned. The period interior is calm and spacious, and there are several displays of glassware, porcelain and furniture. Just don't turn up on Thursday or Friday because it's closed.

A few moments' walk from the cathedral is the Haunch of Venison, probably the oldest inn in Salisbury. It boasts a solid pewter counter and its very own ghost, not to mention the mummified hand of an unfortunate gambler who ended up getting it chopped off during a card game. Back in 1320 it was a hostelry for craftsmen who'd come to work on the cathedral, but now it serves quality dinners and a huge selection of single malts and fine brandies. It's also supposed to have been a brothel in the later parts of the fourteenth century, with its own tunnel into the cathedral quarters, so the clerics could get their end away without being spotted!

THE FIVE TRILITHONS

The horseshoe of trilithons at the centre of Stonehenge is unique in that all of the 15 stones that were erected to form it are still there, albeit some in pieces where two of the mighty gates have fallen. The five units are arranged in a horseshoe shape, about 45 feet across, open towards the north-east. The one positioned at the north-east edge is the smallest, being a 'mere' 20 feet, while the largest would have been the 24-foot trilithon positioned at the south-west edge. This one is known as the Great Trilithon. Only one upright of this still stands; it reaches 22 feet into the sky.

The trilithons are constructed just like the ring of stones, using mortise and tenon joints to fix each lintel in place, but each three stones forms a free-standing structure, and, unlike the outer uprights, the uprights of the trilithons are placed so close together that it would be impossible for anyone to pass between them, leading to speculation that they were used as sighting devices. As with the outer circle, the smoothest side of each stone faces inwards.

HERE, THERE AND EVERYWHERE

Ancient man built stone circles and erected megaliths all over
Europe, including the following sites:

Weris, Belgium	**Hayar Qim**, Malta
Perla Cromlech, Bulgaria	**La Taula de Talatá**, Menorca
Mali Sweto Andeo, Croatia	**Borger**, Netherlands
Filitosa, Corsica	**Istrehågan**, Norway
Langballe, Denmark	**Wietrzychowice**, Poland
Jõelähtme, Estonia	**Montemor Novo**, Portugal
Carnac, France	**Römerschanze**, Romania
Cygnus, Germany	**Sa Perda Pinta**, Sardinia
Spina, Italy	**Pais Vasco**, Spain
Ferschweiler, Luxembourg	**Hjortsberga**, Sweden
Son Oms Vell Sanctuary, Mallorca	**Chavannes-des-Bois**, Switzerland

QUOTE UNQUOTE

*Spectators at the ceremony usually present a mixture of students,
cyclists, hitchhikers from London, couples in evening dress, and a
few youths, perhaps, who manage somehow to camp all night
within the Circle, even though the official gates are closed.*
Dorothy Gladys Spicer, author, writing in
Yearbook of English Festivals, 1954

TWENTIETH-CENTURY DRUIDS

When Druidism was revived again, in Cornwall in the early twentieth century, the first Gorsedd (Gorseth in Cornish) wasn't held at Stonehenge, but at the stone circle at Boscawen-Un, near St Buryan in Cornwall. The first meeting, in 1928, was presided over by Pedrog, Archdruid of Britain at the time and used the ceremonies devised by Edward Williams in London, 100 years earlier. But it was really the brainchild of three supporters of all things Cornish: Henry Jenner, a Cornish native who worked as assistant keeper of manuscripts at the British Museum and was a key figure in the movement to revive spoken Cornish, Robert Morton Nance, whose parents were Cornish, but who was actually born in Wales, one of Jenner's converts, and a Sussex schoolteacher called ASD Smith, who took up the cause of Cornish nationalism because he felt at home there. Perhaps the secluded nature of the site appealed, but more likely it was the fact they wanted to promote Cornwall. Boscawen-Un is well documented as a site of Druidic worship in ancient times.

A VERY BARBAROUS MONUMENT

July 27th 1835

From Salisbury I made a short détour to see the celebrated Stonehenge, of which I daresay Preble will give you a more vivid description out of Worcester's Geography than I can do, although I have seen it so lately. In fact, a very barbarous monument (in the matter of the fine arts at least) has no particular interest when one has seen the much older monuments of much older nations, which preceding ages have only been able to gape at and admire without even being able to imitate, much less to equal. Stonehenge is merely a rude and rather awkward grouping together of about a score of huge and shapeless stones. It may have been a Druid's temple or Queen Boadicea's drawing-room for aught that I (or I believe any one else) know to the contrary, and I can't find enough interest in the grotesque monuments of a parcel of barbarians to detain me from the continuation of my tour. I shall turn it over to the antiquaries.

George William Curtis,
The Correspondence of John Lothrop Motley, 1889

CASTING THE RUNES

Which of the following is not an explanation that has been
put forward for why Stonehenge was built?
a) As a fortress
b) As a seasonal calculator
c) As a lunar temple
d) As a women's sexual cycle calculator
e) As a Druidic temple
Answer on page 153.

THE 'TABLE OF METAL'

According to Tudor legend a strange metal table 'as it had beene tinne and lead commixt, inscribed with many letters' was found buried somewhere near Stonehenge during the reign of Henry VIII, although details are few and sketchy. William Camden in his *Britannia* notes that the inscription was indecipherable by the finest linguists at the time, even though it was sent up to London for examination, and that the table was then lost. Given Henry VIII's sense of self-worth, and a fondness for Arthurian overtones in courtly behaviour, it's surprising no one seemed to make the connection to the Round Table of King Arthur.

Number of the stone in the Avebury stone circle on which the midwinter sunrise falls at Midwinter solstice

STUNNING SITES

There are thousands of ancient sites to visit across the world, on every continent. If you doubt us, look at the list below...

Serpent Mound, Canada
Xinjiang Uygur Autonomous Region, China
Wassu Circles, Gambia
Al Kerak, Jordan
Melaka, *Malaysia*
Waitapu, New Zealand
Pescadores Wall, Taiwan
Dougga Dolmen, Tunisia
Los Ajos, Uruguay
Etowah Mounds, USA

MAKING MOLEHILLS OUT OF MOUNTAINS

If you ask 30- or 40-somethings to name a film which features Stonehenge, 99% of them will say *Spinal Tap* (or *This is Spinal Tap*, to give it its full title). Rob Reiner's hilarious spoof documentary – 'or Rockumentary, if you will' – follows a fading spandex metal band on an ill-fated tour of America. The film draws on many of the legendary acts of excess carried out by heavy metal bands, but pays particular homage to Ozzy Osbourne's old band, Black Sabbath, the fathers of the genre.

In an effort to reinvigorate their performance Spinal Tap decide to revive one of their old 'fantasy' numbers, 'Stonehenge', and their manager is dispatched to get an 18-foot replica of one of the trilithons made by a props artist, around which some dwarves have been hired to dance. Unfortunately when drawing the design on a napkin in haste, someone puts " instead of ', resulting in an 18-inch-high model and one of the most excruciatingly funny scenes as the band attempt to keep going as it is lowered onto the stage.

As the lead singer David St Hubbins, played by co-writer Michael McKean, remarks afterwards: 'I do not, for one, think that the problem was that the band was down. I think that the problem may have been, that there was a Stonehenge monument on the stage that was in danger of being *crushed* by a *dwarf*. Alright? That tended to understate the hugeness of the object.'

Their manager protests he's making 'too big a thing out of it', to which bassist Derek Smalls (played by co-writer Christopher Guest) ripostes 'Making a big thing out of it would have been a good idea.'

LEGENDARY BUILDERS

The giants

There are several different accounts of the building of Stonehenge that
are connected with giants. Geoffrey of Monmouth says the stones
originally came from Africa but were transported to Ireland by a race
of giants, from whence Merlin purloined them and set them up by
magic on Salisbury Plain. In fact, one of the earliest drawings of
Stonehenge shows Merlin as a giant erecting the monument.

The leaning, uneven nature of the stones has suggested the forms of
giants to many people and an alternative name for the henge is the
Dancing Giants. In this case, they were supposed to be supernatural
footloose, fossilised beings who'd been turned to stone when caught
by the rays of the sun – rather like vampires, giants and dwarves
were often supposed to shun the sun.

STOLEN STONES

If you lived on Salisbury Plain and wanted to build a durable house, you
were in trouble. The Plain sits on chalk which is crumbly, porous and
inclined to break under even the slightest stress. Here and there in
the chalk you might find some flint nodules, but you'd be lucky if you
found any more than a foot in any dimension, and most would be much
smaller. So it's not entirely surprising that some locals looked towards
Stonehenge for building supplies.

Sarsen was particularly desirable. Because it was so hard it was very
difficult to work but was extremely durable. We know that most of the
Wiltshire Sarsens wound up broken up and used for surfacing roads
in the early nineteenth century – Scotsman John Loudon MacAdam
demonstrated the value of building hard-surfaced, durable roads made
of crushed rock and gravel over a solid stone bed to speed up the
transport of goods, people and mail when he was made trustee of the
Bristol turnpike in 1816, and his ideas quickly took off. No one knows
if any or many of the missing Stonehenge Sarsens were turned into
turnpike roads, but it's not an unlikely fate. We do know that just after
Inigo Jones conducted his survey of Stonehenge in the seventeenth
century, a large stone was removed and broken up to make a bridge.

In 1977 the Society of Antiquaries published the results of a survey of
the pattern of Sarsen stone occurrence in Wiltshire. The survey showed
an anomaly in the area around Amesbury, but not as many as you would
expect if they were part of a naturally occurring deposit. Therefore, it
was concluded that these extra Sarsens had been taken from Stonehenge
some time in the Middle Ages.

ENTERTAININGLY NAMED BANDS YOU'VE NEVER HEARD OF...

...who played the Stonehenge Free Festival

Androids of Mu
Deaf Aids Killer Hertz
Doll by Doll
Elsie Steer and Cosmic Dave
Flux of Pink Indians
ICU Lightning Raiders
Lighting by Shoe
Man to Man Triumphant
Ozric Tentacles
Popular History of Signs
Psycho Hamster
Stolen Pets
The Wystic Mankers

QUOTE UNQUOTE

It is sobering to reflect that the sarsen monument at the heart of Stonehenge was little more than a century old when the first Labyrinth was raised at Knossos in 1,930 BC.
Rodney Castleden, author, writing in *The Knossos Labyrinth: A new View of the 'Palace of Minos' at Knossos*

ALL FALL DOWN

The first record we have of the fall of any of the stones that make up Stonehenge comes from 1797. On 3 January several people ploughing fields about half a mile from the monument felt the ground quake. This was the result of the south-west trilithon and its lintel falling outward following a heavy snowfall which had thawed rapidly, destabilising the ground. The uprights struck a bluestone, and the lintel rolled off and hit one of the outer Sarsen uprights. There had been reports that local gypsies, stopping for shelter among the stones, had also dug a hole the previous year on one side of the stone, to provide better shelter from the elements.

This event proved of great interest to local antiquarians, who were most surprised to see quite how shallow the stones had been embedded in the ground. It seems they had expected as much of the stone to be under the surface as above it, rather than three to three and a half feet, with more than 20 feet visible above.

Everything you need to know about the restoration work undertaken at Stonehenge in the twentieth century:

Date: 1901

Supervisor: Prof William Gowland
By order of: Society of Antiquaries

Affected: Stone 56
Problem: Stone 56 was leaning at a 60-degree angle
Solution: Stone was straightened and reset in concrete after the pit into which it was sunk was carefully examined and recorded

Date: 1919-1926

Supervisor: Lieutenant-Colonel William Hawley
By order of: Society of Antiquaries/Ministry of Works

Affected: Stones 6, 7 and their lintel
Problem: Both stones were leaning dangerously
Solution: Lintel was removed and stones 6 and 7 supported while the pits beneath them were excavated. Stones 6 and 7 were straightened and cemented in place, and the lintel replaced finally in 1920

Affected: Stones 1 and 2, and 29 and 30, and their linking lintels
Problem: All stones were leaning dangerously
Solution: As above

Date: 1950-64

Supervisor: Profs Richard Atkinson, Stuart Piggott and Dr JFS Stone
By order of: Ministry of Public Buildings and Works/
Society of Antiquaries

Affected: Stones 57 and 58
Problem: Trilithon had fallen
Solution: Trilithon was re-erected and its lintel replaced, after careful study of records, using the original pit as guide, in 1958

Affected: Stone 22
Problem: Stone had blown down during the great gale of 1900
Solution: Stone was re-erected using documentary evidence to ensure that it was placed correctly in 1958

Affected: Stone 60
Problem: Single stone had fallen
Solution: Stone was re-erected in 1959

Affected: Stones 53 and 54
Problem: Stones were tilted at a precarious angle
Solution: Stones were straightened using documentary evidence to ensure they were placed correctly in 1964

48 *Number of the bluestone which would have been hit by the shaft of light through the trilithon when Stonehenge was built*

The Rollright Stones, Oxfordshire

STONEHENGE STREET NAMES

Here are 10 London locations where stone circle enthusiasts will feel right at home.

- The Circle, NW2 • Druids Way, Bromley
- Stone Grove Court, Edgeware • Stonecutter Street, EC4
- Lithos Road, NW3 • Druid Tower, SE14
- Headstone Road, Harrow • Temple Grove, NW11
- Avebury Court, N1 • Salisbury Walk, N19

VAST BARROWS

What would first impress an ordinary wayfarer is the vast number of the round barrows compared with the rarity of those of the older form. The mounds clustered in the immediate neighbourhood of Stonehenge many times outnumber all the long barrows in Britain. Three hundred still exist in an area of twelve square miles; and from one spot hard by the great stones Stukeley counted a hundred and twenty eight. Again, while the long barrows almost always stand on conspicuous hills, round barrows are sometimes placed on low ground. In certain maritime districts, for instance Cornwall and Brittany, it has been noticed that the monuments of the dead are most thickly strewn in the extreme west, as if the builders had desired that the spirits of those who had gone before them might look upon the setting sun.

T Rice Holmes, *Ancient Britain and the Invasions of Julius Caesar,* 1907

Nabta Playa, Egypt

In the middle of the Nubian Desert, 500 miles south of Cairo, lies the remains of the earliest Neolithic settlement in Egypt, and the oldest stone circle identified so far. About 5,000 years ago, when the locals decided to drag chunks of quartzite sandstone over half a kilometre to build the stone circle, the large depression held a lake, and the nomadic people who clustered around it during the summer created a small circle of uprights that measured about four metres in width. It contained two stone 'gates' and two long lines of megaliths on a north-south axis and an east-west axis, probably to help mark the summer solstice; this was 1,000 years before the first stones were raised at Stonehenge. Nearby cairns and other burial mounds, dating from as early as 6,500 BC, contain the bones of cattle, possibly sacrificial offerings.

Little is known about the people who built this circle, although they had lived within the area for millennia before erecting the structure. Digs around Nabta Playa have revealed grain and pottery, and the bones of cattle, suggesting a semi-agrarian people who brought their cattle to the lake in summer to drink, as well as the remains of hares and gazelles that they hunted. The remains date back to somewhere between 8,000 BC

and 11,000 BC. Evidence of later periods suggests that by around 7,000 BC, larger settlements had been constructed. These settlements had permanent houses and a wide range of cultivated crops. Compared to other settled areas in the region, the people of Nabta Playa were more advanced and organised.

These settlements were first discovered in 1974 by Professor Fred Wendorf from the Southern Methodist University in Texas. One of their most puzzling discoveries is a selection of structures, the use and meaning of which remain obscure, about a kilometre from the stone circle and cattle barrows. Over an area 200 x 500 metres, a number of smaller oval stone circles about five by four metres are delineated by a mix of rough and shaped stones, with one or two large slabs laid inside each oval. The curious thing about these ovals is that each one is placed over large, mushroom-shaped table rocks two to three metres beneath the surface. How the ancient people of Nabta Playa knew where to place them, and why, is a mystery. The field of ovals has one more unusual aspect, a hole nearby which is about six metres in width and is dug down to the table rock beneath. A stone sculpture of a cow or other bovine animal has been buried there facing north.

THE SEVEN WONDERS OF ENGLAND

Near Wilton sweet, huge heaps of stones are found,
But so confused, that neither any eye
Can count them just, nor Reason reason try,
What force brought them to so unlikely ground.
To stranger weights my mind's waste soil is bound,
Of passion-hills, reaching to Reason's sky,
From Fancy's earth, passing all number's bound,
Passing all guess, whence into me should fly
So mazed a mass; or, if in me it grows,
A simple soul should breed so mixed woes.

Sir Philip Sidney, *The Seven Wonders of England*

11 FAMOUS VISITORS TO STONEHENGE

Charles II, British ruler and orange-fancier
Sir Winston Churchill, British Prime Minister
Henry James, American author and professional Englishman
Ralph Waldo Emerson, American philosopher and inventor
Horace Walpole, British Prime Minister and aesthete
William Morris, designer, writer and typographer
HG Wells, futuristic writer and war game inventor
GK Chesterton, wit and lover of paradoxes
Charles Darwin, scientist and worm-fancier
Samuel Pepys, diarist and cheese-burier
John Wesley, methodical God-botherer
William Cobbett, jailbird reformer and agriculturist

GOING TO ANY LENGTHS

When it comes to rows of stones, the alignments closest to Carnac in France are the longest, the most intricate and the most impressive yet discovered – it can take up to a day just to view the rows of standing stones, let alone the rest of the erections. The version of Arthurian legend common in Brittany is quite distinct from the Arthurian cycles we're used to and has more in common with the earliest legends of Arthur in Welsh writings such as *The Mabinogion*. Breton legends say the stones were the ranks of invading Roman legionnaires, turned to stone by Merlin. Surrounding the main alignments are numerous menhirs, dolmens and other grave sites. In short, it is the most spectacular destination for those who have an interest in the early history of mankind. The fact that it also happens to be in a picturesque corner of Brittany, with great beaches, restaurants and loads of other history nearby can't hurt when considering a trip to the Quiberon peninsula.

FIVE DIFFERENT KINDS OF BLUESTONES

The bluestones at Stonehenge – which aren't terribly blue – are made up of five different kinds of rock; four are thought to come from the Preseli Mountains in Pembrokeshire, the nearest destination where most of them occur. This range was discovered by the geologist HH Thomas, when he tested a series of samples in 1923.

1. **Dolerite** – bluish green and spotted (except for three stones which are of the unmottled variety)
2. **Volcanic ash** – dark green
3. **Rhyolite** – dark blue green
4. **Calcareous ash** – greyish
5. **Cosheston sandstone** – reddish (from around Milford Haven)

QUOTE UNQUOTE

The ancient astronaut theory claimed that many of the deities worshipped by ancient people were in fact ET visitors.
The argument usually relied on claims that many impressive buildings, such as the Great Pyramid at Gizeh, stone relics of the Incas and the Mayas, or Stonehenge, were constructed under the influence of ET visitors.
David Lamb, author, writing in *The Search for Extraterrestrial Intelligence: A Philosophical Inquiry*

STONEHENGE WAS BUILT BY...

A Swiss nobleman

According to a theory publicised by *New Scientist* magazine in 2003, the ancient monument may have been built by a nobleman from Switzerland or Bavaria.

This Alpine hypothesis depends on analysis of the remains of a wealthy nobleman known as the Amesbury Archer. His grave lies three miles south of the stone circle and was excavated in 2002. Archaeologists discovered that the archer, whose interment they estimate dates to around 2,470 BC, had been buried with the oldest gold and copper ornaments ever found in Britain. This has led to speculation that the man may have been wealthy enough to have paid for the construction of Stonehenge itself.

Further surprises emerged from an analysis of the Archer's tooth enamel. This revealed that he had grown up in a far colder climate than England – probably in the Swiss or German Alps. 'It's a spectacular find,' commented archaeologist Mike Pitts.

OTHER ANCIENT SITES TO VISIT AROUND STONEHENGE AND AVEBURY

Stonehenge cursus – a mile-long Neolithic earthwork just north of Stonehenge.

Woodhenge – an early Bronze Age formation of wooden posts, two miles east of the cursus.

Silbury Hill – the largest prehistoric man-made mound in Europe. It was built around 4,300 years ago.

West Kennet Long Barrow – an Early Neolithic multi-chambered burial mound open to the public, a short walk from Silbury Hill.

Harestone Down – a stone circle close to East Kennet Long Barrow, with good views of Silbury Hill.

Langdean Bottom – remains of a stone circle or hut.

Churchill – one of the few villages in the world that can boast its own trilithon arch.

Lyneham Long Barrow – the chambers of the barrow itself are in poor condition, but it features a large standing stone outside. Visible from the A361 between Burford and Chipping Norton.

Wansdyke – running from Marlborough to Bristol, the area around the dyke was supposed to be a centre for Odin worship.

Falkner's Circle – single stone remains of a circle, near to Avebury.

CHIP OFF THE VERY OLD BLOCK

It's quite hard for us to imagine what the tourists visiting Stonehenge in Tudor times would have seen, because we know a lot of things have been disturbed since then. We also have conflicting accounts of what the monument looked like at various periods during its history. Today, only about half the stones are still standing. Apart from the fallen ones, from which we can conjecture the layout, quite a number have been taken over the centuries to be broken down and used in other buildings or to cobble farm tracks.

If that wasn't bad enough, it also used to be common for visitors to bash and batter their favourite megalith until they had managed to chip off a suitable chunk of rock as a souvenir or a good luck charm. The local blacksmith at Amesbury did a roaring trade hiring out hammers to amateur geologists. Ralph Waldo Emerson, describing a visit to Stonehenge in the late nineteenth century in his *Essays and English Traits*, noted, 'On almost every stone we found the marks of the mineralogist's hammer and chisel'.

For a long time the Greek explorer, Pytheas of Marseilles, was given as the earliest source of writing about Stonehenge. He visited Great Britain around 325 BC, having heard about the tin mining taking place in Cornwall, and is the first person to call the people living there Britains (or Pritains, since he referred to the land as the Pretannic Isle). First landing near Land's End, he then sailed up the English Channel as far as Kent, looking for the source of the Baltic amber trade, which was very lucrative at the time. More misplaced searching led him to circumnavigate Great Britain looking for the mythical land of Thule to the north. On this journey he describes seeing a great stone circle, but historians now believe it was the circle at Callanish in the Outer Hebrides.

DRUIDS OF A SORT

Within recent years the date of the erection of Stonehenge, the last example in time of the British stone circle, has been fixed at about the year 2,000 BC. This is at least eighteen hundred years prior to the first literary mention we possess regarding Druidism, and if we are to connect the two we must imagine a Druidism flourishing at a period considerably older than the building of Stonehenge, than which the majority of our stone circles are greatly more ancient. Mr Kendrick makes a half-hearted plea for the more recent construction of Stonehenge in the earlier La Tene Age, which extended from 500 BC to AD 100. With equal half-heartedness I find myself unable to entertain it. I must admit a constitutional fondness for lost causes, but there are some pricks against which it is fruitless to kick. Nor do I think it worth print and paper to discuss a problem already disposed of, so far as such disposition is possible, by the ablest archaeologists of our time. All I care to add on this question is that it has always appeared to me as not improbably that some form of belief resembling Druidism, some early and evolutionary type of that faith, may possibly have been associated with these circles, and that the Druidic grove may have been a later development of them, or, perhaps, a return to an earlier form of them, such as we find in Woodhenge, on Salisbury Plaine, where tree-trunks took the place of rough stone pillars, and which appears to have been erected, judging from the pottery discovered on its site, at much the same period as Stonehenge.

Lewis Spence,
*The Magic Arts in
Celtic Britain*, 1995

MORE FAMOUS VISITORS TO STONEHENGE

John Evelyn, 22 July 1654
William of Orange, stopped off on his way to his coronation
Cosimo III de' Medici, Grand Duke of Tuscany
Celia Fiennes, late seventeenth century
St John Clerk, 1727
Jonathan Swift, 1730
James I, 1620
Thomas Carlyle
William Gladstone, 1853
Queen Victoria, (she came incognito)

LEGENDARY BUILDERS

The Devil

The Christians had a few goes at sublimating the ancient legendary origins of Stonehenge by superimposing some of their own values on older stories. In one, the Devil goes to an old lady and buys the stones that make up the monument, and carries them off, by black magic of course, to Salisbury Plain, where he erects them in a series of circles. Being a devilish fellow, he decides to play a trick on the locals, and challenges them to guess how many stones he has used. A friar answered him with: 'That is more than thee cans't tell'. A correct – if somewhat oblique – answer. The devil is so angry at being outwitted that he picks up a stone and throws it at the friar. It struck him on the heel, but so strong is the power of God that the friar's heel dented the stone, which now lies where it rebounded, toppled over, and is known as the Heel Stone for this reason.

HEALING PROPERTIES

The stones of Stonehenge were renowned for their healing properties. Layamon, writing in the twelfth century in *Brut*, noted:

> *Magic powers they have*
> *Men that are sick*
> *Fare to that stone;*
> *and they wash that stone*
> *and bathe away their evil.*

According to local legend a whole variety of illnesses and wounds could both be healed by water that fell first on the stones, then on to the sufferer.

Stanton Drew, Avon

The stone circles just outside the village of Stanton Drew are so large that it's difficult to appreciate them unless you obtain an aerial view. This, combined with their out-of-the-way location, means that they don't attract anywhere near as many visitors as their more famous cousins at Avebury and Stonehenge. It also means that they feel untouched, with no gift shops or modern intrusions to take away from the atmosphere. They're signposted off the obscure B3130, south of Bristol, but are barely promoted by the owners, who charge a modest fee for you to trample through their fields, and keep their cows among the stones.

The Great Circle, which is 113 metres wide and is made up of 27 widely-spaced fallen stones plus an avenue, is the second-largest stone circle in Britain, after Avebury. The Northeast Circle, a mere 30 metres across, is also significant. It consists of just eight stones now, with others aligned outside creating the remains of an avenue. A third, smaller circle lies to the south-east, but is not accessible to the public. There are many individual stones scattered about the area – hence its name: Stanton comes from Anglo-Saxon, meaning stone farm.

John Aubrey noted the existence of these stone circles back in 1664, and William Stukeley drew a detailed plan of them in 1776. However, there is no record of excavation at Stanton Drew until 1998, when an English Heritage magnetic geophysical survey found signs that once upon a time large wooden posts made a series of concentric circles within the main ring of stone, ranging in diameter from 95 metres down to 23 metres, and making it the most complex wood structure yet discovered. The survey also discovered that the site of the Great Circle was once enclosed by a seven-metre-wide ditch which had an overall diameter of 135 metres, and an entrance facing north-east.

When the Northeast Circle was surveyed, four rectangular pits were discovered, which lined up with the eight stones of the circle, but it was impossible to tell from the scanning whether these pits might once have held stones, or were dug for a ritual use.

In the nearby village is a group of standing stones called The Cove. All are thought to date from around 2,500 BC. Later legend claimed that The Cove and the stone circles were all guests at a wedding who were turned to stone by the Devil who played the fiddle so they could dance on a Sunday – a common variant of the usual folk motif where sinners are turned to stone for being ungodly.

*Tom regretted that he hadn't taken seriosuly the
rumours of giants on Salisbury Plain...*

CASTING THE RUNES

What's the difference between a dolmen and a barrow?
Answer on page 153.

BEFORE THE STONE AGE

Stonehenge seems so ancient that it's hard to imagine the Wiltshire
landscape without it. And yet, in cosmic terms at least, Stonehenge has
been on the Earth for the merest of moments – a few seconds in the
history of the planet. Stonehenge stands on a 300-square-mile chalk
plateau, part of massive chalk downlands that spread all over southern
England. The same chalk formation gives us the Isle of Wight and the
White Cliffs of Dover. These great chalk deposits were created under
the sea by the shells of huge numbers of prehistoric invertebrates during
the Upper Cretaceous period (not surprisingly, since *creta* is Latin for
chalk!) and then rose up around the same time the Alps were formed,
somewhere between 100 million and 65 million years ago. Ancient
though the scene may seem, centuries before, the whole area was
shrouded in forest. Gargantuan pines and hazel trees closely covered
the expanse we now know as Salisbury Plain.

Nazca, Giza, Machu Piccu, Stonehenge, and Easter Island. And there remains a mystique about each of these, for we do not know, precisely, how their construction was accomplished. There are theories, some more plausible than others, but we do not know.
Douglas E Cowan, religious academic, writing in
Cyberhenge: Modern Pagans on the Internet

PREHISTORIC MAN

The first evidence of *Homo erectus* in Britain dates back to around 700,000 years ago, when the country was still linked to mainland Europe by a causeway. He would have lived in small bands of hunter-gatherers, moving around over a large area to gain sustenance. Around 500,000 *Homo heidelbergensis* also appeared. Both populations are thought to have died out during the Anglian Age. Man next put in an appearance in the warm interglacial period between 420,000 and 360,000 years ago, where he started manufacturing large numbers of flint tools. There is evidence that primitive man may have clung on during the next ice age, possibly because advances in tool technology made hunting easier and survival, therefore, possible, but there is little evidence of occupation during the next warmer interglacial period – at which time Britain first became cut off from Europe.

It wasn't until 30,000 BC that we see the first signs of *Homo sapiens* in the British fossil record, but again ice ages seem to have driven them back to the continent a number of times. The first distinct signs of advanced activity, known as the Creswellian industry, is dated to around 12,000 BC. At this point, not only were groups using bone, shells and animal horn for tools in addition to flint, but they were also using substances such as amber in order to create decorative items.

During the Mesolithic period, around 6,500 BC, melting glaciers cut Britain off from the Continent permanently. The warmer climate meant pine and alder forests thrived, as well as the hardy birch tree. Elk, deer and boar liked the shaded environment of the woodland, and were the main sources of meat for a population that still relied largely on hunting. Man spread into the far north of Scotland, and began to settle down – there is increasing evidence of permanent shelters from the middle of the eighth century BC. But the increase in population brought on by better conditions would force early man to look at new ways of living.

ICONIC

The ICONS project is inviting people to vote on what they regard as symbols of Englishness – objects, activities, places, but no people. The Welsh, Scots and Irish may get a look-in later, if more funding becomes available, but for the moment, this website-led project (www.icons.org.uk) has selected 12 representative icons, and has been asking for opinions and nominations since the beginning of 2006. Will Stonehenge survive the vote? Very probably, when you look at the full list:

1. Stonehenge
2. Blake's 'Jerusalem'
3. Holbein's portrait of Henry VIII
4. *The King James Bible*
5. Punch and Judy
6. A cup of tea
7. *Alice's Adventures in Wonderland*
8. The Spitfire
9. *SS Windrush*
10. The Routemaster bus
11. *The Angel of the North*
12. The FA Cup

STONEHENGE WAS BUILT BY...

The Egyptians

More ink has been expended attempting to prove that whoever built the Great Pyramids of Egypt also had a hand in Stonehenge than for any other theory. Complex mathematical formulas, multiple surveys, lunar and stellar angles have all been called upon as evidence of the synchronicity between the structures. Martin Doutré, author of *Ancient Celtic New Zealand*, confidently claims: 'Whoever built Stonehenge was utterly conversant with the age-old mathematical formulas, geodetic navigational systems, astronomical methodologies and measurement standards found upon the Giza Plateau of ancient Egypt.' And he's certainly not alone – the idea goes back centuries.

According to Count Maudet de Penhouet, writing in 1805, during the well-documented mass exodus from pre-Dynastic Egypt, people were attracted to the better farming conditions of Western Europe and travelled across France, erecting the Grand Menhir at Brisé, in Brittany, and placing the 3,000-plus stones at Carnac as a geographical code. The serpentine forms identified by Stukeley were taken to be symbols from Egyptian hermetic philosophy, or of an ancient serpent cult.

SHORTAGE OF STONES?

The lack of large Sarsen stones now remaining in the Marlborough Sarsen fields, from which experts think it most likely the huge Stonehenge Sarsen uprights were sourced, have led archaeologists and petrologists to consider whether or not the builders of Stonehenge actually ran out of their first choice of building material, and had to look further afield to procure other stones.

A survey of earlier Neolithic monuments in the area which uses large Sarsen stones, such as the large circle at Avebury and a number of chambered barrows, suggests that hundreds, perhaps even a thousand, large Sarsens had already been removed and used before the builders at Stonehenge began even laying out their plans.

CASTING THE RUNES

In the 1950s and 1960s Alexander Thom, joined forces with Gerald Hawkins to found the science of archaeoastronomy – the study of the astronomical beliefs and systems of ancient civilisations. But what were the professions of the two men?

a) Astronomer and historian
b) Astronomer and engineer
c) Both astronomers
d) Chartered surveyor and historian

Answer on page 153.

BEEN THERE, SEEN THAT

Next day we made a party to Bristol hot wells, and added to our company a Miss Scott, of Newcastle, a very pleasing young woman, who afterwards married an eminent lawyer there; and another lady, whose name I have forgot, who was a good deal older than the rest, but was very pleasant, and had £30,000, by which means she became the wife of one of the Hathorns. This place appeared to me dull and disagreeable, and the hot wells not much better. Next day we dined at Dr Gusthard's, and the day after set out on our return to London. We resolved to go by Salisbury Plain and Stonehenge, as neither of us had ever been there, both of which raised our wonder and astonishment, especially Stonehenge; but as we were not antiquarians, we could not form any conjecture about it. We got to London next day before dinner.

Autobiography of the Rev Dr Alexander Carlyle, Minister of Inveresk: Containing Memorials of the Men and Events of His Time, 1861

60 *Number of thousands of man-days Gerald Hawkins estimated that it took to shape the stones of Stonehenge*

BEST WEBSITES

'Best' is a relative term when it comes to Stonehenge. There are an awful lot of websites repeating the same, often erroneous information, plus a lot of extremely entertaining ones which theorise as to who the builders were, what the construction methods were and the purpose of the henge. Here are some of our favourites...

home-3.tiscali.nl/~meester7/engatlantis.html – for more information on how the UK is really Atlantis... very entertaining

myweb.tiscali.co.uk/celynog/index.htm – a site dedicated to megalithic walks – if reading this book has piqued your attention, this is the place to seek advice

witcombe.sbc.edu/earthmysteries/EMStonehenge.html – detailed explanation of the different phases of construction

www.aboutstonehenge.info – the oldest Stonehenge site on the net

www.christiaan.com/stonehenge/index.php – a practical educational guide covering everything from organising day trips to building your own model of Stonehenge

www.eng-h.gov.uk/stoneh/start.htm – English Heritage's site all about carbon dating the henge, for the scientifically minded out there

www.english-heritage.org.uk – the official last word on all things Stonehenge

www.icons.org.uk/theicons/collection/stonehenge/biography/stonehenge-biography – the ICONS project's easily digestible introduction to all things Stonehenge

www.le.ac.uk/archaeology/rug/image_collection/hier/bi – Clive Ruggles, an archaeologist, has been hard at work assembling a collection of images of ancient buildings worldwide; impressive

www.megalithic.co.uk – detailed maps and visitor reports on thousands of ancient sites that you can contribute to

www.mkzdk.org/carnac/stones.html – haunting pictures of Carnac

www.stonehenge.co.uk – a stone-lovers resource, practical info on where to stay and how to visit, photos and recollections of celebrating the solstice there

www.stonehengeusa.com – America's Stonehenge website, nicely illustrated and organised

'What monstrous place is this?' said Angel.

'It hums,' said she. 'Hearken!'

He listened. The wind, playing upon the edifice, produced a booming tune, like the note of some gigantic one-stringed harp. No other sound came from it, and lifting his hand and advancing a step or two Clare felt the vertical surface of the structure. It seemed to be of solid stone, without joint or moulding. Carrying his fingers onward he found that what he had come in contact with was a colossal rectangular pillar; by stretching out his left hand he could feel, a similar one adjoining. At an indefinite height overhead something made the black sky blacker, which had the semblance of a vast architrave uniting the pillars horizontally. They carefully entered beneath and between; the surfaces echoed their soft rustle; but they seemed to be still out-of-doors. The place was roofless. Tess drew her breath fearfully, and Angel, perplexed, said 'What can it be?'

Feeling sideways they encountered a tower-like pillar, square and uncompromising as the first; beyond it another, and another. The place was all doors and pillars, some connected above by continuous architraves.

'A very Temple of the Winds,' he said.

The next pillar was isolated, others composed a trilithon; others were prostrate, their flanks forming a causeway wide enough for a carriage; and it was soon obvious that they made up a forest of monoliths, grouped upon the grassy expanse of the plain. The couple advanced further into this pavilion of the night, till they stood in its midst.

'It is Stonehenge!' said Clare.

'The heathen temple, you mean?'

'Yes. Older than the centuries; older than the d'Urbervilles!... Well, what shall we do, darling? We may find shelter further on.'

But Tess, really tired by this time, flung herself upon an oblong slab that lay close at hand, and was sheltered from the wind by a pillar. Owing to the action of the sun during the preceding day, the stone was warm and dry, in comforting contrast to the rough and chill grass around, which had damped her skirts and shoes. 'I don't want to go any further, Angel,' she said stretching out her hand for his. 'Can't we bide here?'

'I fear not. This spot is visible for miles by day, although it does not seem now.'

'One of my mother's people was a shepherd hereabout, now I think of it. And you used to say at Talbothays that I was a heathen. So now I am at home.'

Thomas Hardy,
Tess of the D'Urbervilles,

Stonehenge in the 1600s, W Camden Britannia

STONEHENGE WAS BUILT BY...

Buddhists

William Stukeley, the noted antiquarian from the eighteenth century, is famous for arguing that the stone circle was the work of Druids. But Stukeley's theory, as first published, was actually more subtle than that; he also believed that the Druids got their knowledge of construction, and some of their design ideas, from the East, and in 1740 he suggested that there were definite similarities between the monument and the Buddhist temples of India. By 1900, the notion that the builders of Stonehenge were well acquainted with Buddhism was considered respectable enough to be mentioned in *Chambers's Encyclopaedia*.

The problem with archaeology is when to stop laughing.
Dr Glyn Daniel, archaeologist

WORST FILMS FEATURING STONEHENGE

1. *Halloween III: Season of the Witch* (1982)
Barmiest *Halloween* spin-off. It has got nothing to do with a knife-wielding maniac. Instead, it is actually about a twisted toy manufacturer (and his army of androids) who plans to use chips of magic monoliths from Stonehenge, embedded in Halloween masks, to unleash the evil Celtic powers of something or other... Frankly awful.

2. *Merlin: The Return* (1999)
Merlin uses the power of Stonehenge to vanquish the evil Mordred and put Arthur and his knightly posse to sleep, just in case Mordred pops up again. Lo and behold, thanks to a crazy scientist in the twentieth century, he does...

3. *Fiddlers Three* (1944)
A pair of sailors take a Wren to Stonehenge, which happens to be a giant time machine, and get catapulted back to the court of King Arthur with, one suspects, supposedly comic consequences. Old-fashioned malarkey.

4. *Puma Man* (*L'Uomo Puma*) (1980)
A UFO drops a gold mask on Stonehenge, which has many useful properties if you're a wannabe world dictator (as Donald Pleasance, in this instance happens to be). The only rain cloud in sight is that it's protected by Puma Man...

5. *Shanghai Knights* (2003)
Comedic adventure yarn. The character played by Owen Wilson winds up crashing an out-of-control prototype racing car into the henge.

6. *Knights of the Round Table* (1953)
Creaky courtly adventure, with Arthur gathering his knights at Stonehenge to hold a primitive parliament and to receive a lecture from Merlin about how Stonehenge is there to remind them of the law of the land.

7. *Valiant* (2005)
Animated feature from the creators of *Shrek* about homing pigeons. Features a lot of English clichés and some flying over Stonehenge.

8. *National Lampoon's European Vacation* (1985)
After winning a tour package on a game show, the bickering Griswald family carve a trail of destruction through England (where they knock over Stonehenge).

Year in the nineteenth century when the Wiltshire Archaeological Society was refused permission to investigate Stonehenge

St Martin's Church, Fifield Bavant

Similar to Britain's oldest pub, the identity of Britain's smallest church causes a stir among those people who find themselves living adjacent to any likely contender. While there are undoubtedly smaller buildings occasionally used for worship – such as the church at Bremilham, also in Wiltshire, which is only 12 feet across – the simple, rectangular Norman church at Fifield Bavant, with its modest tower and tiny windows, can claim to be the smallest in regular use, at just 33 feet long.

Fifield Bavant is located on the Ebble River, between Salisbury and Shaftsbury. The church can easily be reached on foot from the village.

ABC, AS EASY AS 123

The first person to formally set out a division of prehistory into periods was Christian Jurgen Thomsen, a young historian from Denmark. In 1818, he proposed that early history be divided according to the tools and artefacts used by ancient man, thus creating a Stone Age, followed by a Bronze Age and, finally, an Iron Age.

Antiquarians from Scandinavia accepted his categorisation first, but it took several decades for the idea to catch on in other countries. Some of the best evidence in support of Thomsen's categorisation was found in the records of Wiltshire barrow excavations. Of the 151 barrows that had been opened near Stonehenge, only two had iron objects, which was down to the fact that it was an older, existing burial site that was being reused. The majority contained cremated remains commonly found in what

were now to be known as Bronze Age burials; nearly one third contained bronze artefacts.

By the 1860s, Thomsen's dating system was becoming accepted in Britain and it seemed to prove that Stonehenge couldn't have been built after the Bronze Age. But since most of the barrows contained neither bronze nor iron implements, the possibility remained that it was far older. Neither possibility was acceptable to some eminent men, though, and many argued Bronze Age barbarians could not have created something quite as grand as Stonehenge. Daniel Wilson, a Scottish antiquarian, confidently wrote in 1863 that it was, 'certainly not the work of the Stone Period, and probably not of the Bronze Period, with the exception of its little central circle of unhewn monoliths'. In less than one hundred years we would know he had things back to front.

SPOOKY STONEHENGE

The mysterious tank

One of the most reliable sightings of an inexplicable object near Stonehenge occurred in 1957, when the London Garrison took on the Royal Guards from Liverpool in a tactical exercise in Salisbury Valley, near the monument. The London Garrison were equipped with five tanks. While preparing for the start of the exercise, one of the tank crew saw a strange, silvery, cigar-shaped object described as 'tank-like'. He pointed it out to the rest of the crew and prepared to open fire, but then it seemed to disappear, leaving no trace on the ground. After the exercise, no record of a cigar-shaped vehicle being involved in the manoeuvres could be found.

QUOTE UNQUOTE

I was struck only with a general sensation of stupendousness. I had seen prints and read of it so much that there was little novelty. Mr. Brompton accounted for the stones being raised by telling me that they raise immense stones in the East Indies by making a bank of earth, rolling them up it, and then taking away the earth.
Diarist James Boswell's observations for 21 April, 1775

THE GREAT GALE

The night of 31 December 1900 saw a gale sweep across Salisbury Plain, knocking over Sarsen stone 22, and its lintel, 122. The lintel smashed so violently that one of the chunks catapulted 81 feet. The fall attracted a lot of interest – by now Stonehenge was a major tourist attraction – and Sir Edmund Antrobus, the owner at the time, had to pay a policeman to control the gathered crowds.

As a result, Sir Edmund took concerns about safety at the monument seriously. He decided to have it checked over. But even so, he was anxious the local council or national bodies should not interfere with his actions. He only accepted expert help on the understanding it would make no difference to his status as absolute owner of Stonehenge. He decided to fence it off and charge admission. He blocked off the cart tracks that passed through the henge, and in May 1901 put up the fence. In the first six months 3,770 visitors paid to gain entry. Not everyone liked it. There were worries the safety work and restoration would turn out to be unsympathetic; locals claimed they had a right of access to the tracks that crossed the henge; many felt Stonehenge was a national treasure, not one man's private monument, and everyone should have access to it for free.

Year in the seventeenth century when John Aubrey first found the Aubrey Holes

MERLIN

Six centuries, twice told, are now complete,
Since Merlin liv'd on this terrestrial seat.
Knowledge appear'd but dawning to my sight;
She blaz'd on Newton with meridian light.
Yet the faint glimm'rings which my genius taught,
Beyond the ken of human art were thought.
What I by mere mechanic pow'rs achiev'd,
Th'effects of magic, then by most believ'd.
To Stonehenge let the sons of art repair,
And view the wonders I erected there;
Try, if their skill improv'd, mine e'er can foil;
Restore the giant's dance t'Hibernian soil.
Nor in geometry excell'd alone;
But other sciences to me were known.
I study'd Nature through her various ways;
And chaunted to this harp prophetic lays.
To Cader Ydris oft I took my way;
Rose with the sun, toil'd up th'ascent all day;
But scarce could reach the mountain's tow'ring height,
E're radiant Vesper usher'd in the night.
The summit gain'd, I sought with naked eye,
To penetrate the wonders of the sky.
No telescopic glass known in that age,
To assist the optics of the curious sage.
Though lov'd astronomy oft charm'd my mind,
I now erroneous all my notions find.
I thought bright sol around our globe had run,
Nor knew earth's motion, nor the central sun.
And had I known, cou'd I belief have gain'd,
When Ignorance and Superstition reign'd?
Unseen by me, attraction's mighty force,
And how fierce comets run their stated course;
Surprising scenes! by Heav'n reserv'd in store,
For its own fav'rite, Newton, to explore.
With faculties enlarg'd, he's gone to prove
The laws and motions of yon worlds above;
And the vast circuits of th'expanse survey;
View solar systems in the Milky Way.
My spirit too through ether wings its flight,
Discov'ring Truths deny'd my mortal sight;
Transported, hovers o'er my native isle,
Where arts improve, and Peace and Plenty smile.

Ann Finch,
British Women Poets 1660-1800: An Anthology, **1713**

*Year in the twentieth century when timber structures and large 67
quantities of bones were found at Durrington Walls henge*

DEATH IN THE CIRCLE

Only four bodies have ever been found buried within Stonehenge's stone circle, although many more lay in barrows in the immediate vicinity. Here's what happened to the four.

1. The famous decapitated man, probably executed by the Saxons using a sword, unearthed in 1923 but lost from 1941 to 1999. Dated to between 600 and 700 AD.

2. The only other complete skeleton to come to light is of a man who died in a hail of arrows. He was unearthed in 1976 in the ditch.

3. Parts of a body thought to be Roman, about which almost nothing is known. The parts were reburied at Stonehenge in 1922.

4. Parts of a body were found in 1926 towards the centre of the circle. It was thought at the time to be contemporary with its building. Sadly, the bones have been lost.

CASTING THE RUNES

William Stukeley believed the earth monuments around Stonehenge, including the circle at Avebury, West Kennet Avenue and Beckhampton Avenue, made up the shape of which animal?
Answer on page 153.

WOODHOUSE PARK – THE OTHER STONEHENGE

For a brief time in the late nineteenth century, Londoners didn't have to go to the trouble or expense of travelling to Wiltshire to enjoy the majesty and grandeur of Stonehenge. All they had to do was take themselves off to Shepherds Bush in West London, where they could see a full-size replica of 'Stonehenge as it was' at Woodhouse Park.

Opened in 1894, the park offered many entertaining sights for just sixpence – the owners put on recitals, concerts and lectures, and the intrepid could even go 1,000 feet up in a fixed balloon ascent. Despite this, not enough members of the paying public came, and the plan to create a companion reconstruction, 'Stonehenge as it is', never materialised. Within a few years the henge was gone, and in its place stood a power station.

...according to www.megalithic.co.uk, whose reviewers rate the circles for overall condition, ambience and ease of access. Scotland is so rich in well-preserved Neolithic monuments that only those scoring 12 or more out of 15 are listed.

Auchagallon, Isle of Arran, 15
Stenness, Orkney, 15
Balnuaran of Clava NE, Highlands, 14
Torhousekie, Dumfries and Galloway, 14
Balnuaran of Clava Centre, Highlands, 13
Balnuaran of Clava SE, Highlands, 13
Marionburgh, Moray, 13
Achavanich, Highlands, 12
Ardlair, Aberdeenshire, 12
Balbirnie, Fife, 12
Carse Farm 1, Perth and Kinross, 12
Croft Moraig, Perth and Kinross, 12
Cullerlie, Aberdeenshire, 12
Deer Park, Aberdeenshire, 12
Easter Aquorthies, Aberdeenshire, 12
Glassel, Aberdeenshire, 12
Image Wood, Aberdeenshire, 12
Loch Buie Stone Circle, Isle of Mull, 12
Machuinn, Perth and Kinross, 12
Parkneuk, Perth and Kinross, 12
Rothiemay, Moray, 12
Strichen House, Aberdeenshire, 12
Tomnaverie, Aberdeenshire, 12

HEEL AND TOE

Supporters of the astronomical interpretation of Stonehenge, that it was an observatory used to predict astronomical events like eclipses, had long been puzzled by the function of the Heel Stone, since the sun does not rise above it on midsummer morning. The old explanation was that the rising sun's bottom hit the stone once it had risen a bit and was passing across the sky, or that it was involved in lunar calculations.

A chance discovery in 1979 altered that. Repairs being done to the verge near the Heel Stone revealed a second hole, similar to that which held the Heel Stone. Some suggested it was once the original hole dug for the stone, others have taken it as proof there was once a companion rock to the Heel Stone, now gone. Numbered 97, the position of the hole shows the pair of stones would have framed the rising sun accurately.

One is tempted to ask how it is that the Romans, masters of the world, came and disappeared, whilst the race of the rude constructors still remains...
James Miln, antiquarian

BEST OF BRITISH

Castlerigg Stone Circle, Cumbria

Long regarded as one of the most important stone circles in Cumbria, Castlerigg is also one of the most visually impressive. The circle itself is thought to date from the late Neolithic, around 3,200 BC. It measures 30 metres across, and is made up of 38 stones which sit on top of a low hill and look out over Lonscale Fell, Skiddaw and Blencathra. The changeable Lake District weather ensures the stones never look quite the same two days in a row. From the surrounding hills you can get spectacular vistas of the layout of the circle, and indeed see that it's not terribly circular, having one flattened side. Currently it attracts several thousand visitors each year, especially in the summer.

Within the circle are a further 10 standing stones in the eastern corner. These are up to 3.2 metres tall and form an enclosed area or cove, the purpose of which is unknown. Like so many stone circles, the arrangement of the ring of stones seems to be of astronomical significance.

The stones themselves are not worked, and not one in the circle is over five feet tall. An axe head was found there in 1875, but further excavations in 1882 only uncovered quantities of charcoal, rather than any hoped-for items of archaeological significance. In 1913, when a parliamentary act first gave the state real powers to care for monuments of national importance, Castlerigg was bought by a group led by Canon Hardwicke Rawnsley, who would go on to co-found the National Trust. As a child he wanted to grow up to be an Arctic explorer, and although founding a heritage organisation may not seem as romantic, in the long run he did a great deal more good.

For those who are interested in strange phenomena, it should be noted that the Castlerigg Stone Circle was also the site of an early UFO sighting. In 1919 a Mr T Singleton was observing the circle with a friend when they both saw several white balls of light passing slowly over the monument. Some people think that the lights are a natural phenomenon – perhaps what caused the original builders to choose the site they did.

Around 4,500 BC, at the beginning of the Neolithic period, people began to practise small-scale farming alongside their traditional hunter-gatherer way of life. By this time the climate had warmed and mixed deciduous forests, or oak, birch, elm and hazel had replaced the pine forests and tundra grasslands of the end of the preceding Ice Age.

Domesticated animals, pigs, sheep and cattle, and cereals such as wheat and barley were part of a package of farming that had spread across Europe before finally arriving in Britain. Farming, even on a small scale meant settling down in small groups, but the change in diet did not necessarily bring about any increase in life expectancy and living alongside your animals can cause problems of disease. Most people probably did not live much beyond 40, but there would have been some who did survive and their great age must have given them great status. Clothing was most probably of hide, there are beads of bone and stone and the first simple pottery was produced. With life tied to the seasonal calendar of the agricultural year, people banded together to build communal structures such as hill-top enclosures and burial mounds for their ancestors. These long earth mounds, houses for the dead, reflect the shape of the houses of the living.

Life was not isolated, the evidence from stone axes shows that they were traded over great distances and although life on the whole seemed to be peaceful there is, even in these early times, evidence of conflict over land.

LOCAL MUSEUMS WHERE STONEHENGE ARTEFACTS CAN BE FOUND

1. Salisbury and South Wiltshire Museum (The King's House, 65 The Close, Salisbury, Wiltshire SP1 2EN, www.salisburymuseum.org.uk, tel 01722 332151). Contains an award-winning Stonehenge gallery.

2. Wiltshire Heritage Museum (41 Long Street, Devizes, Wiltshire SN10 1NS, www.wiltshireheritage.org.uk, tel 01380 727369). Extensive collection of Neolithic and early Bronze Age artefacts excavated from the barrows around Stonehenge.

3. Ashmolean Museum of Art and Archaeology (Beaumont Street, Oxford OX1 2PH, www.ashmol.ox.ac.uk, tel 01865 278000). Houses objects dug up by Lieutenant Colonel William Hawley during his investigation of the site for the Ministry of Works in 1921-1928.

The first self-appointed custodian of Stonehenge was Henry Browne, who from 1822, when he moved to Amesbury, started haunting the stones and offering his services to visitors as a guide and historian. The Marquis of Queensbury and later Sir Henry Antrobus gave him permission to officially act as a guide and keep any tips he received, in return for keeping an eye out for any bad behaviour. Browne reportedly never did very well from his tours, but he did succeed in selling several cork models of Stonehenge. They came in pairs, 'before' and 'after', and sold for seven guineas. Browne's attention to detail was amazing. He fastened his models together with small nails, attaching them to a base covered in green fabric to simulate grass. Curious artisans can see one that was made about 1824 and originally bought by Reverend William Richards, Rector of Chevenell in Wiltshire, in the Ashmolean Museum, Oxford, along with many of Browne's watercolours, also painted to sell to tourists.

As well as attending to visitors to the ancient site, Browne also walked long distances to give lectures on his take on ancient history, summed up in his book *The Geology of Scripture*. And an entertaining, if misguided, take it was. Browne believed Stonehenge was an antediluvian temple, pre-dating the flood God used to wipe out undesirables, which only Noah survived. It was this flood, he told listeners, that had swept down upon Wiltshire from a south-westerly direction and this accounted for the damage to the stones in that direction; they had borne the brunt of the impact of the water. Browne was one of the last believers in Catastrophism, a theory that attempted to marry Darwin's discoveries about evolution with the Biblical account of the creation of life, by admitting to the veracity of fossils but trying to fit all of the stages geologists had thus far discovered into less than six centuries, meaning God could still have created the Earth in 4,004 BC. Unfortunately Browne embraced this theory just as the last few fashionable proponents were quietly forgetting about it

Browne also published several apocalyptic tracts with any spare money he had, and shortly before his death walked all the way to London, pushing one of his Stonehenge models on a handcart, intending to present it to the British Museum. Unfortunately the doormen wouldn't let him in, and he returned home dejected, dying soon after in 1839. He was succeeded by his son, Joseph, who spent more than 40 years as 'attending illustrator' to the stones.

Joseph preferred to stay close to Stonehenge and concentrate on tourists rather than spreading the word of the impending apocalypse, which perhaps explains why he made a better living, selling copies of his father's guidebook and his own artworks, and lecturing on the antediluvian temple until he was too old to work. He was able to retire with the help of friends.

Incised Markings on a Stone, Northumberland,
J Collingwood, 1869

THE GREAT MELTING CIRCLE

But we have something still better, namely an evidence of the mixed civilisation which grew out of the contact of invaders and invaded and implies some association between them. That is Stonehenge, the largest of the megalithic monuments. The Goidels must have provided the religious idea, their predecessors the method of construction. The grouping of a large number of round barrows about the monument, its successive transformations, revealed by the latest excavations, its constant use until after the Roman conquest, and, lastly, the ancient tradition of a circular temple of the Sun among the Celts of the Ocean, all compel one to ascribe its construction to the first Celtic occupants of Britain. It implies the highest degree of power and organisation of which prehistoric times have left a trace. It has, too, been thought that the great number of barrows surrounding Stonehenge proves that men came from far away to be buried near the holy place. These funeral pilgrimages would demand roads, such as the well-known Pilgrims' Way, a prestige as a sanctuary, and a social unit of vast extent and influence, something like the great Goidelic Kingdom of Britain, the memory of which has been preserved, but post-dated, by tradition.

MR Dobie, Henri Hubert, Raymond Lantier, Jean Marx,
Marcel Mauss, *The Rise of the Celts*, 1934

ASTERIX IN STONE

Asterix is one of France's most enduring comic book heroes, a tiny Gallic warrior fighting to stop the invading Romans from conquering his village, the only bit of Armorica Julius Caesar hasn't overrun. This is mostly due to Asterix being able to gain immense strength by drinking a special potion brewed up by the village Druid, Getafix (or Panoramix in French). Asterix's best friend, Obelix, was dunked in it as a baby and has grown up good-natured, and almost as strong as he is stupid. Created by artist Albert Uderzo and writer René Goscinny, 31 volumes have appeared since 1961.

One of the running gags in the series of *Asterix* stories is the rewriting of history to include Asterix and Obelix in significant events. In *Asterix in Spain* (where Asterix also accidentally invents bullfighting), Stonehenge is explained as a redevelopment project undertaken by Unhygenix the Fishmonger, who's got his eye on Salisbury Plain. He agrees to lend Asterix his boat in return for the super-strong heroes transporting some menhirs for him, explaining how the giant stones were erected.

In a similar vein, Obelix is responsible for breaking the nose off the Sphinx in *Asterix and Cleopatra*, and Asterix introduces tea to the British – who are drinking hot water with milk in it until he comes along with some herbs given to him by the druids in *Asterix in Britain*.

BLASTED BURROWERS!

Stonehenge has withstood wars, climate change, acid rain, low-flying aircraft and even music festivals, albeit with the assistance of a few tons of concrete. But the latest force to threaten the integrity of the monument is rather cuter: the elusive badger. Nocturnal creatures, badgers clearly aren't put off by the hordes of visitors who trample through the area by day. At night, when it's peaceful, they find the soft chalky downland perfect for digging their burrows, disturbing the remains of millennia that lie, in some cases, just inches below the surface. They seem to like the long barrows in the Stonehenge area, with about half of these Neolithic burial sites showing signs of badger activity, and in the last three years several have been abandoned to the badgers because they have already caused so much damage.

Archaeologists have found the best way to keep badgers off is to wait until the set is empty, then set up a wire fence around it to prevent them returning. Badgers often dig more than one set and, if prevented from using one, simply amble off to another.

CASTING THE RUNES

Avebury is the biggest megalithic monument in the world, in terms of area. But what is the circumference (to the nearest hundred feet) of the 1,401-foot diameter circle?

Answer on page 153.

WORTH TO THE WORLD

Stonehenge and its surrounding area (including Avebury) was declared a World Heritage Site in 1986 by the United Nations Educational, Scientific and Cultural Organisation (UNESCO). Such designations are decided by a committee made up of representatives from 21 of the member states, who are each elected for up to six years (although most step down after four to allow more members to participate), making sure a range of worldwide voices is heard.

Historically Europe leads the way in World Heritage status, with countries such as France and the UK having more designated World Heritage Sites than those as large as Australia or Russia. In 1994, however, an initiative to make sure the selection process was diverse and representative was launched – the Global Strategy for a Balanced, Representative and Credible World Heritage List. At the time, only 90 World Heritage Sites were of natural interest compared to 304 of cultural interest.

The idea of an overseeing body protecting places of cultural, architectural or historical significance to everyone became popular in the late 1950s, when the builders of the Aswan High Dam in Egypt proposed flooding the valley containing the Abu Simbel temples. Fifty countries got together and donated over US$80m to the appeal to save the temples. As a result of UNESCO's intervention the temples were taken apart and reassembled in another location to preserve them. After several more interventions, UNESCO got together with the International Council on Monuments and Sites (ICOMOS) and together they drafted a convention to protect the world's cultural heritage. It wasn't until 1972 that UNESCO took on the role of protecting significant habitats as well. The Convention Concerning the Protection of World Cultural and Natural Heritage was adopted by UNESCO on 16 November 1972.

Only places in countries who have signed up to the World Heritage Convention can be nominated – and each member country has an 'inventory' of its most important sites known as its Tentative List, from which sites are nominated for World Heritage status. UNESCO currently has 34 sites on its danger list, including those in areas where there is civil unrest, a breakdown of infrastructure or threat to the environment.

In ancient times, hundreds of years before the dawn of history,
an ancient race of people... the Druids. No one knows who they
were or what they were doing...
On-stage song introduction for 'Stonehenge'
from the film *This is Spinal Tap*

MEGALITHS DU MONDE

The Pescatore Walls, Taiwan

In the seas off the Pescatores (or Peng-hu) islands between Taiwan and China may lie the remains of one of the oldest man-made structures ever recorded. Taiwanese diver Steve Shieh first discovered signs of man-made structures on the ocean bed there decades ago, having been asked by a local government official to keep an eye out for proof that legends of a large red castle that had once stood in the area and was buried beneath the waves were true, while conducting other dives. Shieh spotted the first of what have been described as 'walls' off the island of Hu-ching 30 years ago, but it was only in September 2002 that more significant ruins were found off the coast of Tong-chi Island – walls hundreds of metres in length, half a metre thick and up to three metres high that crossed at right angles. Signs of a city layout were also identified.

The ruins have been dated to between 6,000 BC and 12,000 BC (although one paper reports Japanese researchers as having dated them between 10,000 BC and 80,000 BC!). One theory suggests that the walls weren't built by the race we know as the modern Chinese, who migrated to the area around 6,000 BC, but are remains of an older, previously unknown civilisation, and that the city was submerged when sea levels rose during an ice age around 9,600 BC. Megalithic scholars have been comparing the Chinese find to evidence of an ancient city found beneath the seas off Yonaguni-jima in Japan.

Originally, the area was a peninsula of mainland China, around 13,500 years ago. It later became an island and then further seismological activity reduced it to 64 smaller islands, supporting the ruined castle theory. However, some scientists such as Professor Tsao Nu-ching from Taiwan's Central Geological Society suggest the structures could be natural, caused by volcanic eruptions which 'can also create linear formations, due to the inherent joints and planar structures'. In other words, liquid lava can be forced into cracks in existing rocks, which then wear away forming towering sheets of rock which resemble walls.

NOTABLE PEOPLE WHO HAVE
DUG UP STONEHENGE

How apt that among the latest investigators
Mr Stone was followed by Mr Pitts!

Richard Cunnington (1798, 1810)
Richard Colt Hoare (1810)
William Gowland (1900)
William Hawley (1919-1926)
Robert Newell (1919-1926)
Stuart Piggott (1950-1964)
Richard Atkinson (1950-1964)
John FS Stone (1950)
Mike Pitts (1989)

OWNERS THROUGH THE AGES

Amesbury Abbey – Stonehenge was part of the land owned by the nunnery, which was supposedly founded some time after 928 by Queen Elfrida in atonement for her part in the murder of her son-in-law Edward II, who became known as Edward the Martyr.

Edward Seymour, Duke of Somerset – to whom it was given as part of a 20,000-acre estate by Henry VIII after the dissolution of the monasteries in 1540.

Robert Newdyk – purchased the Amesbury estate around 1614.

Sir Lawrence Washington – bought the estate in 1628 from a debt-ridden Newdyk and handed it down through the family for 50 years. Washington was an ancestor of American president George Washington.

The Reverend Thomas Hayward, – obtained it from the Washington family, and received a Royal Warrant to hold a fair there in 1680 (or 1690).

The Bruce family – settled by marriage on the Bruce family who were Earls of Aylesbury.

Lord Carleton – bought it from Lord Charles Bruce in 1720.

Charles, Duke of Queensberry – was left the estate in 1725 by his uncle, Lord Carleton.

The Antrobus family – bought the estate in 1824, and sold it when the family's only direct heir was killed in World War I.

Cecil Chubb – bought it for £6,600 at an auction during World War I, then gifted it to the nation in 1918.

The only contemporary writer who makes mention of the British Druids is the Roman historian Tacitus, who recorded Suetonius Paulinus's campaign to subdue Britain in 60 AD. The general marched through Wales to the island of Anglesey only to have to return when news of Boudicca's revolt reached him. Chapter 30, Book 14 of his *Annals* records that 'women were running through the ranks in wild disorder; their clothing funeral; their hair loose to the wind, in their hands flaming torches, their entire appearance resembling the frantic rage of the Furies. The Druids were ranged in order, with hands raised to the heavens, invoking the gods, and pouring forth horrible curses. The unfamiliarity of the situation struck the Romans with awe and terror.'

The troops, at the urging of their officers, who reminded them what would happen if people thought they were afraid of a bunch of women and religious fanatics, overcame their fear and advanced, and a massive slaughter ensued. The Romans captured the island, long seen as a stronghold of Druidism, and set up a garrison to keep the peace and flush out any Druids. 'The religious groves, dedicated to their superstitions and barbarous rites, were razed to the ground. [It was] in those recesses that the natives [stained] their altars with the blood of their prisoners, and looked for the will of the gods in the entrails of men.'

Notably, Tacitus identifies the Druids as worshipping in groves, not stone structures, barrows, or other ancient monuments.

The Roman view of Druids was not very flattering (but then they were a threat among a barely subjugated populace who might spark an uprising). Apart from Tacitus's mentions of human sacrifice and their methods of divination – it should be noted the practice of reading the future in the entrails of animals by a haruspex was still common in Rome at the time – Julius Caesar also presented a damning portrait. He was speaking of the Druids he encountered in Gaul who, as judges and priests, could condemn a man to death because 'unless for a man's life a man's life be paid, the majesty of the immortal gods may not be appeased'. Caesar noted they sacrificed children, and made mass sacrifices inside a kind of giant man made of twigs – if you've seen *The Wicker Man* you'll get the idea – which 'they fill with living men and set on fire; the men perish in a sheet of flame'.

These sources made it hard for William Stukeley and other proponents of Druidism to present it as a benign religion that promoted knowledge. Stukeley's idea is that the Druids are linked to Old Testament Christianity, and in particular Abraham, which is carried to them by the Phoenicians. They are the keepers of this faith, but, he says, it may have been corrupted by influences from mainland Europe, or they may have misunderstood the story of God asking Abraham to sacrifice his son Isaac.

OLD PICTURE, NEW CAPTION

The Stonehenge kitchen was a modest affair

IMAGINE STONEHENGE IN WAPPING...

Now know that Rome is to me infinitely, cruelly melancholy. *Ipsae periere ruinae*. It is a great unclean charnel house, strewn with the bones of successive generations and types – but a charnel-house, twice ten times desecrated, abused and transformed. The bones are not cast out and strewn, but they are set up in monstrous derision and used with a sort of sardonic wantonness which makes everything a mockery. It is the triumph everywhere of the ignoble over the noble. There must be something grand about the mere absence of every vestige where Babylon stood, there is something touching in a ruin so long as one stone stands upon another in its decay. But fragments of beautiful old buildings, the sites of the most illustrious deeds in the world's history, are neither beautiful, grand, nor touching when they are smothered up in piles of feeble and pompous superstructures, when they are overlaid with infinite filth and tawdry makeshifts and adaptations. Stonehenge is a grand spot, but imagine Stonehenge set down in Wapping, with a gasometer in the middle, two or three of the piers painted and stuccoed up into a Bethesda chapel, a George II. church on the other side, dealers in marine stores under the beams, and the columns placarded with Day & Martin's blacking and a large portrait of Mr. Spurgeon. Stonehenge would lose as a place of interest.

Frederic Harrison, *Autobiographic Memoirs Vol. 1*, 1991

SPOOKY STONEHENGE

The ghosts that roared

The Red Lion pub in Avebury, which is situated in the middle of the Avebury stone circle, has long attracted tales of ghostly goings on. Visitors to the hostelry, parts of which date back to the sixteenth century, have reported seeing a black-draped figure called Flori. Flori's husband returned from the English Civil War and caught her in another man's bed, so he killed them both. Flori is supposed to haunt the inn (specifically its toilets!), looking for a bearded man, presumed to be her lover. Others have reported seeing the ghostly figure of just such a man, sitting beneath the main chandelier, which begins spinning without being touched.

The Red Lion also attracts phantom coaches, with patrons seeing horse-drawn carriages pulling up outside the former coaching inn, and ghostly children have been seen running in the corridors. A Victorian lady in a flowery dress is a regular visitor to the bar area, and poltergeist activity has been reported.

While filming a ghost-hunting TV show, *Most Haunted* in 2002, former *Blue Peter* presenter Yvette Fielding left the pub screaming after five minutes, saying afterwards that she had felt hands in her hair and later found red marks on her back.

ROTTEN SARUM

During the Regency period Old Sarum near Salisbury became notorious as a rotten borough – an area that was allowed to return members of parliament, despite the fact that hardly anyone actually lived there, so there were few voters involved in the process. The person who decided who was voted in was the person who owned the land – this was known as being a 'pocket borough' because it was in someone's pocket.

When Old Sarum first began voting for a local MP, back in 1295, it was a populous town, but by the 1830s there were only three houses there, containing 11 voters, none of whom would have dared go against their landlord's wishes in what was an open ballot. Despite this it returned not one, but two MPs to each parliament, a situation Thomas Payne commented on in his *Rights of Man* in 1791: 'The town of Old Sarum, which contains not three houses, sends two members; and the town of Manchester, which contains upwards of sixty thousand souls, is not admitted to send any. Is there any principle in these things?' In 1832, after 500 years of being a parliamentary constituency, Old Sarum's sway was finally abolished thanks to the Great Reform Act.

DRUID RANKS

Welsh and Breton Druids, and many others, still observe the distinction between three levels of acolyte. If you happen to visit a festival, you can tell them apart by the colour of their clothes. Cornish Druids, more confusingly, all wear blue robes, irrespective of rank.

Archdruids – wear purple robes
Druids – wear white robes
Bards – wear blue robes
Ovates – wear green robes

'THE SPIRIT OF STONEHENGE WAS STRONG UPON ME!'

'To the right or the left?' said I, and forthwith took, without knowing why, the left-hand road, along which I proceeded about a hundred yards, when, in the midst of the tongue of sward formed by the two roads, collaterally with myself, I perceived what I at first conceived to be a small grove of blighted trunks of oaks, barked and grey. I stood still for a moment, and then, turning off the road, advanced slowly towards it over the sward; as I drew nearer, I perceived that the objects which had attracted my curiosity, and which formed a kind of circle, were not trees, but immense upright stones. A thrill pervaded my system; just before me were two, the mightiest of the whole, tall as the stems of proud oaks, supporting on their tops a huge transverse stone, and forming a wonderful doorway. I knew now where I was, and, laying down my stick and bundle, and taking off my hat, I advanced slowly, and cast myself – it was folly, perhaps, but I could not help what I did – cast myself, with my face on the dewy earth, in the middle of the portal of giants, beneath the transverse stone.

The spirit of Stonehenge was strong upon me!

And after I had remained with my face on the ground for some time, I arose, placed my hat on my head, and, taking up my stick and bundle, wandered round the wondrous circle, examining each individual stone, from the greatest to the least; and then, entering by the great door, seated myself upon an immense broad stone, one side of which was supported by several small ones, and the other slanted upon the earth; and there, in deep meditation, I sat for an hour or two, till the sun shone in my face above the tall stones of the eastern side.

George Borrow, *Lavengro: The Scholar – The Gypsy – The Priest*, 1851

AIMS OF THE WORLD HERITAGE
PLAN FOR STONEHENGE

1. A core zone of permanent grassland, freed of roads and inappropriate structures, carefully managed for open access on foot for visitors
2. A high-quality visitor centre outside the boundary of the WHS
3. Access to the stones and the heart of the WHS via drop-off points and 'gateways' on the rim of the core area
4. Access to the wider landscape using the existing public rights of way network and new links to currently inaccessible sites and areas
5. A wider landscape of sustainable, low-intensity mixed farming, with improved conservation and management of important archaeological monuments and ecological features
6. Conserve and enhance the WHS landscape and its many archaeological monuments
7. Increase understanding and enjoyment of the whole WHS
8. Improve the landscape setting of Stonehenge, creating a core area of grass, free of traffic
9. Enhance the nature conservation value of the WHS, especially for the chalk grassland
10. Maximise benefits for the local community
11. Encourage research

(Source: English Heritage)

NOT WHOLLY HOLES

Visitors arriving at Stonehenge for the first time that expect the Aubrey Holes to be, well, holes, may be a little surprised. This loose ring consists of 56 holes, which over the years were used as burial sites and dumps, and filled in, the original purpose of which is still being debated. They are believed to date back to the first phase of construction at Stonehenge, but have been used and reused many times since.

When John Aubrey, the Restoration writer and antiquarian, visited Stonehenge he noticed five indentations in the ground and, being a thorough observer, noted them. It wasn't until much later that the full extent of the holes was realised – Robert Newall was the first person to identify the circle of filled-in pits in his survey of the site in the 1920s. Some authorities, such as Mike Pitts, don't believe Aubrey was even talking about what have now been named the Aubrey Holes in his honour, because the holes had been filled in very thoroughly. He believes what Aubrey observed were five recently made dips from stones that had been removed from the site or from uprooted trees.

WOOD YOU BELIEVE IT?

Woodhenge, so called because it was originally a wooden structure, was probably set up during the Bronze Age possibly for a religious purpose. The concrete posts mark the position of the original timbers. The six concentric rings are indicated in different colours in the plan. The rings are oval with the long axis pointing to the rising sun on Midsummer Day. The red concrete posts (which do not form part of any of the rings) and a burial near the centre are shown in black on the plan. A bank with the ditch on the inner side surrounded the monument, which was entered by a causeway on the NE.

Inscription describing Woodhenge on a plaque in Amesbury during the 1940s and 1950s.

STONEHENGE WAS BUILT BY...

The Greeks

For several centuries scholars have toyed with the idea that the Greeks were somehow involved in the construction of Stonehenge. If looking for an ancient civilisation capable of long-distance travel and formidable architecture they seem a natural choice. Their legends are full of stories of ocean voyagers, while their buildings are still held up as examples of great architecture.

The Society of Antiquaries of London undertook excavations at Stonehenge in 1919 and its findings suggested (to them, at least) that Mycenaean Greeks and Minoan Cretans – whose civilisation flourished during the Bronze Age period from around 3,000 BC to 1,100 BC so the timings do at least broadly fit – had been involved in the construction.

Sir Arthur Evans had only begun his excavation of the six acres of royal palace at Knossos two decades earlier, and before that Heinrich Schliemann had uncovered what he believed to be the palace of Menelaus and Agamemnon, so the Aegean Greeks and Minoans were very much 'in vogue' at the time. Many saw their distinctive decorative style echoed in some of the stone carvings at Stonehenge, but it takes a very liberal interpretation to translate the higgledy-piggledy layouts and ornate and tapering forms so typical of Minoan architecture into the enormous blocks of Stonehenge. The huge stones used to construct the famous palace at Mycenae in the Peloponnese got historians thinking in that direction – the stones were so large that it was supposed to have been built by the Cyclopes, a race of one-eyed giants, echoing the legends of giants building Stonehenge.

Stonehenge as it would have been constructed according to Inigo Jones's belief that it was a Roman temple.

STONEHENGE AFTER WORLD WAR I

Although Stonehenge survived World War I without being torn down as a hazard to low-flying aircraft from nearby airbases on Salisbury Plain, so much activity so close by can't have helped the stability of the stones, which had been deteriorating for years. When Lieutenant-Colonel William Hawley was dispatched by the Department of Works to examine the monument, it was with an eye to restoring the stones, and not to dig up their secrets.

When Hawley arrived, four of the more precariously leaning stones in the outer circle had been propped up with metal posts and pieces of timber for years, while several others were looking unstable. From old records he knew that many of the fallen stones had once stood erect, and he attempted to put things right – somewhat ham-fistedly by modern standards. While Hawley was hitching ropes to the fallen stones and using cranes to reposition them, the barbed wire fence which had enclosed the monument very near to the stones was moved back to keep visitors out of harm's way, and the track across the site was diverted to the west.

MIDSUMMER CELEBRATIONS
IN ANCIENT CULTURES

Many believe Stonehenge was created by ancient Britons as a solar temple or calendar, and that celebrating the summer solstice was an important part of their religious celebrations. Original peoples around the world celebrated the longest day in ways that are often similar.

Celts: Called their midsummer festival Alban Heruin, or 'Light of the Shore' and celebrated by a ritual passage of power from the Oak King, who represents the growing year to the Holly King, who represents the waning one.

Gaul: The Feast of Epona took place in honour of a horse goddess who personified fertility, symbolised by a woman on a mare.

Germany and Slavic countries: Lovers' festival, celebrated with bonfires; people predicted their partners or blessed their union by jumping through the flames – the crops were supposed to grow as high as the biggest leap.

Scandinavia: Norse cultures held 'Things', a kind of parliament-cum-religious-festival, around midsummer, where religious rituals mixed with court functions. Ritual sacrifice was necessary to ensure fertility, and plants picked on this day were thought to have magical powers of healing. Healing springs linked with Odin and Thor were visited. Fires were lit to drive away evil spirits.

Early European Christians: The Feast of St John the Baptist was celebrated over several days at midsummer, often incorporating older pagan ceremonies. It was probably the first feast to be introduced, and is supposed to commemorate his date of birth.

Romans: A week of festivities held in Rome, in early June, in honour of Vesta, goddess of the hearth. During this week, married women were able to enter her shrine and see the sacred flame. At all other times only the vestal virgins, who tended it, were allowed in.

Chinese: Summer solstice was a celebration of the female principal, the force of the yin, connected with the Earth. The winter solstice balanced it by celebrating the masculine yang.

Native Americans: Different tribes had different customs, but sun worship seems to be common to a lot. Many left behind stone monuments that seem to have been built as solar calendars. Hopi Indians believed kachinas, spirits who acted as go-betweens between men and the gods, left their villages to visit the dead in the mountains, and they would dress as kachinas and dance to send them on their way. The Natchez held a ceremony to celebrate the growing crops, and none could be harvested until after the event.

SPOOKY STONEHENGE

Waking the dead

Stonehenge's only well-documented ghosts (well, as well-documented as any ghostly apparitions can be) are thought to be the spirits of Captain B Lorraine and Staff Sergeant R Wilson, whose plane crashed there in 1912. As the first members of the Royal Flying Corps to die in service, they warrant a monument near the henge. Unlike most ghosts though, this pair don't appear as ghostly figures; witnesses have reported seeing their plane in the process of crashing. Sir Michael Bruce was driving past Stonehenge with a group of friends just before D-day when they observed a small plane in difficulty, which appeared to crash land in a nearby wood. On attempting to go to the rescue, all the party found was the memorial to Lorraine and Wilson where they thought the plane had come down.

QUOTE UNQUOTE

On my way I visited Stonehenge – the first place I ever went to see as an object of curiosity, and I had all the enjoyment that was to be derived from so novel and so sublime a scene.
Henry Crabbe Robinson, diarist

REGENCY STONEHENGE

The Regency Era was a time when visiting the stones properly became an acknowledged pastime, when a desire to experience the sublime was at its height. The open plain and ancient monument suited the mood of the period.

Visitors had a choice of how to get there. The nearest thing to public transport at the time was the system of stage and mail coaches which criss-crossed the country. The London to Exeter stage stopped at Amesbury each day, but if you used its service you would then have to put up until the next coach came along, besides possibly hiring transport to the stones themselves. There was also a day tripper's coach which left Salisbury at 3pm three days a week. The better-off could hire a horse or carriage (or bring their own, of course), but this was an expensive option. It did, however, allow a leisurely day taking in the chief local sites, with a picturesque picnic lunch among the monoliths. For a small sum the 'Shepherd of Salisbury Plain', a figure made famous by religious tracts, would come and hold your horses and tell you all about the legends of the place – in fact, several 'shepherds' appear to have been quite forceful in their desire to help. It wasn't until 1822 that the stones had a regular and more informed guardian in the shape of Henry Browne.

Year in the twentieth century in which Stonehenge was declared a World Heritage Site

CASTING THE RUNES

During the nineteenth century, summer visitors to
Stonehenge at the weekends could...
a) Watch a display of trained horses
b) See a dance troupe re-enact Druid ceremonies
c) Take watercolour classes at a special mobile art school
d) Watch the Stonehenge XI cricket team take on all comers
Answer on page 153.

THE MEGALITHIC OLIVE PRESS

When German Saharan explorer Heinrich Barth published his *Travels and Discoveries in North and Central Africa* in three volumes in 1857, he caused many sensations, not least by his account of discovering tall trilithons of carefully worked stones, with a drilled lintel, mounted on a stone-stepped dais into which channels were carved. He immediately decided the trilithons were sundials and possibly also involved in sacrifices – hence the channels for the blood to run off.

Barth's claims didn't come out of the blue, however. There are a large number of megalithic remains in the district, with many fine examples in Tunisia, Morocco, Algeria and so forth. So for several decades, many people had been inclined to believe Stonehenge's builders had originated in the near East and Barth's Phoenician theories revived once more.

However, by the early part of the twentieth century, closer study revealed the trilithons to be, in fact, olive oil presses. T Eric Peet in his book, *Rough Stone Monuments and Their Builders,*

wrote: 'The traveller Barth speaks of stone circles near Mourzouk and near the town of Tripoli. The great trilithons (senams) with holes pierced in their uprights and "altar tables" at their base, which Barth, followed by Cooper in his *Hill of the Graces,* described as megalithic monuments, have been shown to be nothing more than olive-presses, the "altar tables" being the slabs over which the oil ran off as it descended.'

Barth was an intriguing figure not, one suspects, too concerned about the dating of a trilithon close to home in Tripoli. An explorer who had studied many subjects, including archaeology, history and geography at the University of Berlin before going to London to learn Arabic, Barth took part in several notable expeditions from Tripoli to Ghadames, Ghat and Lake Chad. In one instance, having underestimated the amount of effort and water needed to climb a mountain, he slit one of his own veins and drank his blood to quench his thirst and give him enough strength to keep going until his party found him!

DRUID ORDERS WHO MAKE UP THE
COUNCIL OF BRITISH DRUIDS

The Council of British Druid Orders (COBDO) came about after the unrest around Stonehenge in the late 1980s due to the newly introduced Public Order Act. Four Druid orders met, recognising they needed to present a united front. (We like the idea you can be a GOD or a SOD.)

Ancient Order of Druids (AOD)
Glastonbury Order of Druids (GOD)
Order of Bards Ovates and Druids (OBOD)
Secular Order of Druids (SOD)

DRESSING THE STONES

One of the factors that tends to distinguish Stonehenge from other stone circles is the extent to which many of the stones have been dressed (shaped) before being erected. In most British circles – indeed in most worldwide – few or none of the monoliths show evidence of the kind of attention the majority of those at Stonehenge display.

Although the stones do vary in size, they are very carefully placed. The depth to which the Sarsen stones of the outer ring are buried is adjusted to make their tops very close to horizontal. Adjustments in setting them are also made to allow for the gentle slope of the ground. In all cases the dressed stones are set so the smoothest side faces the inside of the structure.

In addition to carving curved surfaces, the builders of Stonehenge also created a dry stone 'mortise and tenon' joint almost unique in the history of stone building. The top of each of the Sarsen stone uprights was carved with two bumps which corresponded to a bowl-shaped indentation carved on the base of each lintel, so two lintels could be securely 'pegged' to the top of each. The ends of the lintels were also carved into 'toggle' joints – a raised, roughly half circular hump running vertically down one of the narrow ends, and a corresponding channel carved out of the other end. Thus the lintels could be slotted into each other and fixed securely. To allow for slight unevenness of the standing stones below, some of the lintels were individually and very finely shaved to make their upper surface as level as possible.

These techniques are more usually seen in woodworking, and have been used to support the theory that Neolithic man was more used to creating henges from wood, the evidence now rotted away, and simply transferred the techniques to stone.

STONEHENGE WAS BUILT BY...

Black giants

One ancient Irish tradition has it that Stonehenge was constructed not by hardworking Celts from southern England, but by a race of black giants from Africa known as the Formorians – 'a mighty race/taller than Roman spears' whose members were the first to settle in Eire after Noah's flood. The Formorians, legend says, had long, twisted hair that resembled snakes, and oozed poison from their hands, destroying everything they touched.

There may even be something in the tradition – stone circles similar in design to the British monument have been found along the Atlantic coast of Africa as far south as Senegal.

QUOTE UNQUOTE

Stonehenge, in the early summer's morning, appeals to me more than any place builded by man. It has a unique expression, and it is mainly expression that gives a scene, an object, its æsthetic value.
WH Hudson, author, writing in *Letters*

RAINY MAJESTY

To Mrs Burne-Jones

'...I was much impressed by it [Stonehenge], though the earth and sky nearly met, and the rain poured continuously, nothing could spoil the great stretches of the Plain, and the mysterious monument that nobody knows anything about – except Fergusson who knows less than nothing.

We went right up the Avon valley, and very beautiful it was; then, as the river narrowed, we turned off towards a little scrubby town called Pewsey that lies in the valley between the Salisbury and the Marlborough downs: it was all fine and characteristic country, especially where we had to climb the Marlborough downs at a place I remembered coming on as a boy with wonder and pleasure: Oare Hill they call it. We got early in the afternoon to Marlborough and walked out to see the College, and so strolled away to the Devil's Den, and back in the dusk. The next morning we set out early for Avebury, in weather at first much like the day before; however it cleared before we reached Silbury, and was quite fine while we were thereabout for two hours, after which we drove on towards Swindon, intending Lechlade and Kelmscott that evening.'

August 1879
William Morris,
The Letters of William Morris to His Family and Friends

...according to www.megalithic.co.uk, whose reviewers rate the circles for overall condition, ambience and ease of access. Only those scoring 10 or more out of 15 are listed.

Hirnant, Ceredigion, 14
Bedd Arthur, Pembrokeshire, 13
Cerrig Duon, Powys, 13
Cerrig Pryfaid, Conwy, 13
Circle 275, Conwy, 13
Druids Circle, Conwy, 13
Four Stones, Powys, 13
Moel Goedog W, Gwynedd, 13
Moel Ty Uchaf, Denbighshire, 13
Tyfos, Denbighshire, 13
Gors Fawr, Pembrokeshire, 12
Eglwys Gwyddelod, Gwynedd, 11
Ysbyty Cynfyn, Ceredigion, 11
Bedd Gorfal, Gwynedd, 10
Bryn Gwyn Stones, Anglesey, 10
Cerrig Gaerau, Powys, 10
Circle 278, Gwynedd, 10
Kerry Hill, Powys, 10
Pen Y Beacon, Powys, 10
Waun Mawn, Pembrokeshire, 10

IF IT'S TUESDAY THIS MUST BE STONEHENGE

Today Stonehenge is a major tourist attraction, bringing three quarters of a million people, half of them foreigners touring the sights of England, to Salisbury Plain every year. As a focus for tourism Stonehenge has a lengthy pedigree that stretches back to Tudor days. Christopher Chippindale, in his excellent *Stonehenge Complete*, is even able to track down the first foreign visitor to spend a day examining the stones.

According to Chippindale, the first tourist was a Swiss Protestant named Herman Folkerzheimer, who was forced to flee when anti-Protestant feelings became elevated while he was studying history and philosophy in Catholic France, in 1562. It took him eight days to sail from La Rochelle to Southampton, and from there he made his way to Salisbury to visit the Bishop's Palace, as he had an introduction to Bishop Jewel. On 20 July, the Bishop took him hunting and then on to see 'some things that would astound me', including the hill fort at Old Sarum and Stonehenge. Bishop Jewel described it to him as a Roman monument, and Folkerzheimer recorded that the Bishop 'cannot see how even the united efforts of all the inhabitants of his diocese could move a single stone out of place'.

To do anything to break the marvellous effect of the lonely plain and great masses of stone would be cruel. The sight is the most impressive in England, and on no account should it be destroyed by a hideous iron railing.

William Flinders Petrie, archaeologist, objecting to plans for Stonehenge in a letter to *The Times* at the turn of the century

BOUDICCA'S TOMB?

Stonehenge has been associated with funeral monuments for some time, and although we now know it was not erected to commemorate any dead king, a legend persisted for many years that the British Chieftain, Boudicca was laid to rest there. Boudicca was famous for leading the Iceni rebellion against the Romans in 60 AD after her husband Prasutagus, a vassal king, willed half his lands to her instead of the invaders. When the Romans tried to take over Iceni territory in Norfolk and Suffolk, Boudicca gathered several Celtic tribes together to form one of the largest armies ever raised to that date in Great Britain, probably numbering over 100,000 men. She certainly proved a fearsome leader whom the Romans didn't forget easily. Two hundred years after her birth, in his *Roman History* written around 230 AD, Cassius Dio Cocceianus described Boudicca as 'Very tall, in appearance most terrifying, in the glance of her eye most fierce, and her voice was harsh; a great mass of the tawniest hair fell to her hips; around her neck was a large golden necklace; and she wore a tunic of various colours...'

While the Roman governor Suetonius Paulinus was busy in North Wales (after those pesky Druids, no doubt), Boudicca's troops burned St Albans and Colchester. Marching on London they slaughtered 10,000 people and burned much of the city – a layer of charred remains can still be seen to this day if you dig down deep enough. But however good the large but seemingly inexperienced army were at taking towns, they proved no match for the orderly might of the Roman legions. Although outnumbered 10 to one, Suetonius's army was able to ambush the Celtic forces, and reportedly slaughtered 80,000 men in one day, with losses of only 400. Even allowing for the fact that the victors write the history, it was clearly a terrible defeat.

Boudicca drank poison after the battle, and according to legend has been buried all over the place. Not only was Stonehenge once believed to be her resting place, but she is also said to rest on top of Parliament Hill and under Platform 8 at London's King's Cross station!

What's the difference between a menhir and a megalith?
Answer on page 153.

BEST OF BRITISH

Pentre Ifan, Nevern, Dyfed

Undoubtedly the most famous and heavily visited prehistoric site in Wales, the tumulus of Pentre Ifan, well signposted from the village of Nevern, which is a few miles from Fishguard, is a small but striking erection. It is thought to date from around 3,500 to 4,000 BC, but the jury is out as to whether or not it was built in one stage or if the tomb part was erected and then the earth mound created to cover it at a later date. As you approach the site, you'll see many standing stones, suggesting a hub of Neolithic activity. The tumulus is also known as Arthur's Quoit, and *Pentre Ifan* itself means 'Ivan's village'.

What is so striking about Pentre Ifan is the way the broad capstone is balanced on three finely tapered uprights, which are about 2.4 metres tall, creating the central chamber of the tomb. All of the rock involved in the construction is local igneous rock. To the south are a pair of 2.4-metre portal stones with a further stone between them. This is probably where the tomb was entered. Unusually, the tomb is orientated north to south, with the entrance to the south and the capstone pointing north. Over the years it

is believed that the earth covering them has eroded away, leaving just the stark stones.

The site was excavated between 1936 and 1937 and again between 1958 and 1959. Based upon these, archaeologists believe there was originally a shallow oval depression with the burial chamber at its base, and over that an earth mound nearly 40 metres long was raised.

The area also seems carefully chosen, overlooking Fishguard bay; some archaeologists have speculated the builders believed the location brought the dead person closer to the sun, which was worshipped as a giver of life, and also much closer to the spirit world. In the nineteenth century, when Druids were still considered to be the most likely builders of Neolithic monuments, many believed that Pentre Ifan was not a tomb at all, but a chamber in which novice Druids were placed for days to meditate, a common activity in shamanistic traditions worldwide. Druidic legend had it that the interior of the tomb was called 'the womb of Ceridwen', a Celtic deity representing poetic inspiration. Meanwhile, local folk tales tell of sightings of a fairy army, wearing red caps at Pentre Ifan.

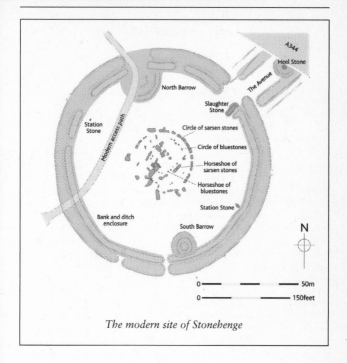

The modern site of Stonehenge

WHILE YOU'RE IN THE AREA WHY NOT VISIT...

The Atwell-Wilson Motor Museum, near Calne

The Atwell-Wilson Motor Museum could be the perfect solution if you're suffering from Neolithic over-exposure, and all those stones are starting to look alike. For people interested in the development of the modern world, the 125 vintage and classic cars on display here, covering the period from the 1920s to the 1980s, offer a nostalgic history of vehicles that changed the face of Great Britain (and most of the world).

There are classic British vintages and great American names, starting with a Model T Ford. It's worth noting that like many attractions in the area, the museum often closes on Friday and Saturday, so check dates carefully before turning up.

Year in the twentieth century when English Heritage commissioned a 93
major consolidation of all known data about Stonehenge

According to Geoffrey of Monmouth's history of Britain, *Historia Regum Britanniae*, several people are buried beneath Stonehenge's monumental trilithons.

1. Ambrosius Aurelianus

Ambrosius Aurelianus was a Roman leader who defended England against the invading Angles and Saxons. Probably. He may have led the combined Roman and Celtic forces at the battle of Mount Badon, and be a paradigm for the legendary King Arthur, but due to the lack of sources during the Dark Ages, historians aren't really sure where Mount Badon is, or even with any certainty in which century the battle took place, much less the definite names of those who took part. It's possible Ambrosius was related to one of the emperors who held power in Rome during this turbulent period. It's also possible that he fought the equally shadowy figure of Vortigern, the British warlord credited with inviting the Angles and Saxons into the country in the first place. By the time Geoffrey gets his hands on him six centuries later, Ambrosius (Geoffrey persistently and incorrectly refers to him as Aurelius Ambrosius throughout the *Historia*) has become the son of a King Constantine and brother of Uther Pendragon.

2. Uther Pendragon

Geoffrey of Monmouth is the first person to make mention of Uther Pendragon, as a son of Constantine who, along with his brother Ambrosius, is sent into exile in Brittany when his elder brother is murdered by Vortigern, and returns to avenge him. In Geoffrey's version, Uther is sent by Merlin to get the huge stones that make up Stonehenge from Ireland, and goes on to sire King Arthur by seducing Igraine, the wife of King Gorlois of Cornwall, while in magical disguise as her husband. Also, in this version, he and Igraine have a daughter, Anna. He gains his nickname because of a standard he has made after seeing visions of dragons.

3. Constantine III

Geoffrey also gave Stonehenge as the final resting place of Constantine III. The historical Constantine was a common-born Roman citizen who rose to become a general of the Roman army in Britain, and declared himself Emperor in 407 AD during a campaign against the invading Germanic tribes. He set up his capital in Arles, now southern France, but his reign lasted only four years. It wasn't until 408 AD that Rome actually recognised him, when the ineffectual emperor Honorius's army had mutinied and deserted him, even then he only became co-Emperor with Honorius. In Geoffrey's version, Constantine was a King of the Celtic Britons and Welsh, brother of the Breton King Aldroenus, who is sent to rule Britain to still the unrest after the death of Gracianus Municeps.

Mysterious rows
Of rude enormous obelisks, that rise
Orb within orb, stupendous monuments
Of artless architecture, such as now
Oft-times amaze the wandering traveller,
By the pale moon discerned on Sarum's plain.
Gilbert West, writer, taken from his poem
'Institution of the Order of the Garter'

POPULARITY CONTEST

The top 10 bestselling books, in reverse order, with 'Stonehenge' in their title, from Amazon.co.uk (on 1 May 2006):

1. *Stonehenge: A Novel of 2000BC*, Bernard Cornwall (Harper Collins)

2. *Sacred Sites of the Knights Templar: The Ancient Secrets Hidden in Stonehenge*, Rennes-le-Chateau and Santiago de Compostela – John K Young (Fair Winds Press)

3. *Stonehenge: Celebration and Subversion*, Andy Worthington (Alternative Albion)

4. *Stonehenge*, Robin Heath (illustrator) (Wooden Books)

5. *The Stonehenge Gate*, Jack Williamson (Tor Books)

6. *Stukeley's Stonehenge: An Unpublished Manuscript, 1721-1724*, Aubrey Burl and Neil Mortimer (Yale University Press)

7. *Arthur & Stonehenge: Britain's Lost History*, Emmet J Sweeney (Domra Publications)

8. *America's Stonehenge: The Mystery Hill Story*, David Goudsward (Branden Books, US)

9. *From Stonehenge to Las Vegas*, Cornelius J Holtorf (AltaMira Press)

10. *Stonehenge: A Teacher's Handbook*, Carol Anderson (English Heritage)

Diameter in metres of the largest of the concentric wooden post circles **95**
that once stood at Stanton Drew

It's very difficult for us to look at the sprawling landscape of Stonehenge, overlaid by millennia of human activity, and imagine what our ancestors saw when they first raised the stones. We bring emotional attachments and interpretations to ancient monuments because of the way they look to us, and modern associations that fundamentally change how we think of the cultures that built them. In the case of Ancient Greece, we see graceful white stone pillars, supremely elegant with their decorative friezes, forgetting entirely that many of their temples would originally have been painted in bright colours. With Stonehenge, we see a softened landscape and moody stones, and it brings up feelings of the romance of ecology, of magic and mystery. The stones themselves are more rounded, some of their surfaces polished by a million footfalls when they would have originally been textured. The Sarsens have stood the test of time, but many of the bluestones are heavily pitted, and their colours have been muted by centuries of moss and moulds.

To the builders of Phase III it must have looked even more imposing, geometric and uniform, with its carefully smoothed surfaces. Looking out from the henge they would see a landscape dotted with shining white barrows and earthworks, stark against the green, not the grassed-over humps and bumps we now know.

CHRONOLOGY

Debate has raged for centuries, and will no doubt continue to rage, as to the precise dating of Stonehenge. Like any generation, we can only state what we know so far. All dates are approximate.

Phase I:

3,000-2,920 BC – Ditch dug by hand, using antler picks to break up the chalk. Bank created from what was dug out.

2,900-2,600 BC – Aubrey Holes dug and used to hold timbers; timber structures built.

Phase II:

2,550 BC – Bluestones arrive from Wales – set up in first temporary arrangement.

Phase III:

2,400 BC – Sarsens arrive and are set up in circle with lintels and horseshoe of trilithons.

2,280-1,930 BC – Bluestones rearranged as circle and horseshoe. Stonehenge complete.

Stonehenge and other ancient monuments aren't the only things that are carefully protected in the area. There are many endangered bird species being carefully looked after and monitored in wildlife sanctuaries and designated areas on Salisbury Plain. These sites include the Royal Society for the Protection of Birds' (RSPB) Normanton Down Bird Sanctuary and the Salisbury Plain Special Protection Area (SPA). Here are just 12 of the many bird species that conserving the land around Stonehenge also protects:

Bittern • Cirl bunting • Corn bunting
Greenfinch • Grey partridge • Lapwing
Pipit • Reed bunting • Skylark
Stone-curlew • Twite • Wagtail

WEIGHTS AND MEASURES

Although Daniel Defoe wrote about ghosts, comets and ladies who gave birth to rabbits, he always had a practical turn of mind, as demonstrated by his less than poetic description of Stonehenge.

These stones at Stonehenge, as Mr Cambden describes them, and in which others agree, were very large, tho' not so large, the upright stones 24 feet high, 7 feet broad, 16 feet round; and weight 12 ton each; and the cross stones on the top, which he calls coronets, were 6 or 7 ton, but this does not seem equal, for if the cross stones weigh'd six, or seven ton, the others, as they appear now, were at least 5 or 6 times as big, and must weigh in proportion; and therefore, I must think their judgment much nearer the case who judge the upright stones at 16 ton, or thereabouts, supposing them to stand a great way into the earth, as 'tis not doubted but they do; and the coronets, or cross stones, at about two ton, which is very

large too, and as much as their bulk can be thought to allow.

Upon the whole, we must take them as our ancestors have done; Namely, for an erection, or building so ancient, that no history has handed down to us the original, as we find it then uncertain, we must leave it so: 'Tis indeed a reverend piece of antiquity, and 'tis a great loss that the true history of it is not known; But since it is not, I think the making so many conjectures at the reality, when they know they can but guess at it, and above all the insisting so long, and warmly on their private opinions, is but amusing themselves and us with doubt, which perhaps lyes the deeper for their search into it.

Daniel Defoe, *A Tour through England & Wales: Divided into Circuits or Journies Vol. 1*, 1928

STARRY SCRIBES

Here are six legendary figures who are supposed to have known about the Glastonbury Zodiac, of which Stonehenge is part, and referred to it:

Homer – unlikely to have been a single person

Hercules – who visited, according to some theorists

Jason – some say his quest on the Argo brought him up the English Channel

Odysseus – who didn't, despite undertaking the original odyssey

Joseph of Arimathea – Glastonbury abounds with legends about him

Perseus – with a flying horse England's practically on your doorstep

QUOTE UNQUOTE

If we cannot save Stonehenge from the Department of Transport then nothing is safe. It is a symbol of British heritage and we would be letting down our predecessors who fought so hard to buy the land roundabout [sic].
Martin Drury, director-general of The National Trust

LEGENDARY BUILDERS

The Atlanteans

According to Plato, Atlantis – a mythical civilisation that sank beneath the waves thousands of years even before he was writing, and whose people were advanced in art and science – was a large island situated outside the Pillars of Hercules, somewhere beyond the Mediterranean and somewhere in the Atlantic. Its capital lay on the southern coast with a large harbour, in a fertile plain, surrounded by mountains.

However, some people believe it didn't sink. In fact, they believe we are living in Atlantis, and that Portsmouth, Exeter or perhaps even Poole was its capital. Plato refers to a 'precipitous' coast approaching the capital, which theorists have identified with the White Cliffs of Dover, and they have even suggested the River Avon's name is derived from Atlantis.

From there, deciding Stonehenge is an Atlantean temple is only a tiny jump. Front-runners for either the remnants or the precursors of the Atlantean civilisation are the Minoans, but close behind them come the monolith-erecting people of the Atlantic coasts, because both races built circular structures. Plato tells us the capital of Atlantis was round, and the other major civilisations all favoured square or rectangular buildings.

How wide was the first circle of stones erected during
the first phase of Stonehenge's creation?
a) 313 feet
b) 330 feet
c) 3,300 feet
Answer on page 153.

SWISS RULE

Originally thought to be a king of the Ancient Britons, the body known as the Amesbury Archer was eventually revealed to have been, in all probability, Swiss, or possibly from Bavaria. He was one of many settlers from abroad who have been identified as the Beaker People.

When originally exhumed by Wessex Archaeology in May 2002, the richness of the man's burial led the press to speculate on his situation in life. Over 100 objects were found in the grave, including the oldest gold objects ever found in Britain, nearly 10 times the usual number for the period. They included copper knives that originated in Spain and France, as well as arrowheads (possibly all that was left of a bow and sheaf of arrows), a leather bracer to protect the arm when firing a bow, boars' tusks, metalwork tools and pottery. Clearly the archer was an important figure.

The body was of a man about five feet nine inches, who died aged around 35-45 years between 2,400 BC and 2,200 BC.

Although powerfully built, his left kneecap had been ripped off by some unknown accident several years before he died, which would have left him with a suppurating wound, and he would have been in constant pain. However, he survived several years, throwing his weight on his right side when he walked. At the time of his death he had a serious abscess in his jaw. Some suggested he may have been a leader involved in the organisation of the building of Stonehenge. Possibly he brought new techniques from Europe, which might explain the uniqueness of the stone circle.

The Amesbury Archer's grave was discovered during a routine archaeological excavation on a housing development about three miles from Stonehenge. Close by, in a separate grave, was the body of a younger man. Aged around 20-25 years, testing suggests that the two were related, possibly father and son. Unlike his father, though, the young man spent his entire life in Britain, although he may have gone to the Midlands or Scotland at some point.

BEERS BREWED BY STONEHENGE ALES

Stonehenge even has its own brewery! Bunces' Brewery, based at the Old Mill, Netheravon, Wiltshire, has been making a fine range of ales using local ingredients since 1984, under the name Stonehenge Ales. Here are its current offerings:

Bodyline (produced for the 2006 cricket season)
Celebration Ale • Danish Dynamite
Great Bustard • Great Dane (lager)
Heel Stone • LTS (Lunch Time Special)
Old Smokey (September to November only)
Pigswill • Rudolph (December and January only)
Second-To-None (June to August only)
Sign-of-Spring (February to May only) • Spire Ale

THE GOOD SHEPHERD

Few people today have heard of Hannah More (1745–1833), but towards the end of the eighteenth century she was a celebrated writer of improving essays and tracts. Everything she wrote contained a strong sense of morality, with titles like *Thoughts on the Importance of the Manners of the Great to General Society*. In 1799, she helped found the Religious Tract Society.

Her most popular homily was *The Shepherd of Salisbury Plain* (1795), based, in part, on the life of one David Saunders of West Lavington. More took the Saunders family as her model of the deserving rural poor. In the tract, a gentleman called Mr Johnson is taking a trip on foot across Wiltshire when he meets the shepherd, who gives him a lively and inspiring account of his life, for which he is rewarded with a half crown. In the second part, Mr Johnson goes to visit the

shepherd at home with his equally pious wife and eight children and, overcome by their godliness, rounds up the local bigwigs to find them a better house and a bigger income.

The Shepherd of Salisbury Plain became quite well known in America. Mark Twain outlined the withering aspirations of the lower middle class by describing their bookshelf as: 'Several books, piled and disposed, with cast-iron exactness, according to an inherited and unchangeable plan; among them, Tupper, much penciled; also, "Friendship's Offering," and "Affection's Wreath," with their sappy inanities illustrated in die-away mezzotints; also, Ossian; "Alonzo and Melissa:" maybe "Ivanhoe:" also "Album," full of original 'poetry' of the Thou-hast-wounded-the-spirit-that-loved-thee breed; two or three goody-goody works – "Shepherd of Salisbury Plain,' etc.'

SET IN STONE

If you're having trouble remembering your cromlechs from your coves, here's a handy guide to some Neolithic features.

Avenue – a formal approachway to a henge or stone circle, its edges defined either by parallel earthwork banks and ditches or parallel lines of standing stones.

Cove – a square or rectangular stone construction, often with little space between the stones and an entrance space to the south-east. Usually found within henges or stone circles.

Cursus – an elongated earthwork enclosure, its sides defined by shallow ditches and low internal earthwork banks. They range in size from as little as 50 metres to several miles and the banks at the ends are generally larger. Their name relates to their original discovery in the eighteenth century when they were thought to be Roman racecourses.

Henge – a circular or oval earthwork enclosure with a ditch and an external bank broken in one, two or occasionally more entrances. The enclosed central area usually contains circular or oval arrangements of upright stones or traces of similar structures in timber.

Megalith – literally, large stone from the Greek *megas*, which means large and *lithos*, which means stone. Any large piece of rock used in the construction of a Neolithic structure. Menhirs are megaliths, as are the constituent parts of Stonehenge, the stones used for many tombs, etc.

Menhir – a single standing stone, from the old Breton for 'long stone'. The largest found would have towered 20 metres into the sky, but is now broken into four pieces.

Stone circle – a variation of the same idea that can be seen enclosed within some henges. Stone circles at a variety of scales can be found wherever there is a suitable source of building material, from Cornwall and Wales to Orkney.

IN THE ROUND

An interesting fact, noted by Michael Dames, author of *The Avebury Cycle*, is that the circle formed by the lintels of the Sarsen circle, were they all in place, is the same diameter (30 metres) as the flat top of nearby Silbury Hill. Both the 167-metre-wide base and the top of Silbury Hill form almost perfect circles. Dames suggested Silbury Hill is a symbolic effigy of a Mother Earth goddess, associated with Lammas, or harvest time, and Stonehenge's third phase of construction was intended to echo this, hence the corresponding measurement.

WHILE YOU'RE IN THE AREA WHY NOT VISIT...

The Battle of Ethandun Memorial

The Battle of Ethandun took place in 878 AD and proved to be the decisive victory in King Alfred's attempts to drive the invading Danish Vikings out of Britain. Without this victory the Saxon kingdoms of Mercia, Wessex, Northumbria and East Anglia would never have united against the common danger.

The Danes, led by Jarl Guthrum, were encamped at Chippenham, while Alfred gathered his levies from Wiltshire, Hampshire and Somerset. The armies came face to face between 6 May and 12 May, on the downs above Edington and Bratton. After a lengthy confrontation, the Danes broke and retreated. Alfred followed them back to Chippenham and, after a two-week siege, accepted their surrender.

You can still see the ancient Sarsen stone that was erected at the site of the battle, which now forms part of the public recreation area at Bratton Castle near Bratton Camp. As well as touring the Iron Age hill fort, we suggest a detour to Edington Priory, built by William of Edington, Bishop of Winchester in the fourteenth century, which looks more like a fortress with its crenellated towers and buttresses.

BALLOON SNAPSHOTS

Before the rather magnificent set of aerial photos documenting the whole area around Stonehenge, which now reside in the Ashmolean Museum, were taken in the 1930s there were several other attempts to get an overhead shot of the area.

Way back in 1900, a local vicar had tried to take a shot from his own balloon (vicars clearly had more exciting hobbies in those days, as well as more generous stipends) but he was so far up that the resultant image is almost useless: Stonehenge is a tiny pinprick. Then, in 1906, a Royal Artillery balloon based at the Larkhill military camp drifted over the site (not entirely to plan, it seems) and took some shots, resulting in the first-ever aerial archaeological images.

William Hawley realised the potential of aerial photos, and tried to arrange for the RAF stationed at Old Sarum to take pictures in 1921. He especially wanted some that would help him trace the path of the avenue. Nothing came of his negotiations, but in 1923 existing negatives were found showing parallel lines running across from Stonehenge to Amesbury – the line of the avenue ditches.

Number in thousands of worked flints found in 750 hectares around Stonehenge

As well as dramatist John Speed, there is another man with an identical name who is linked to Stonehenge – mapmaker John Speed (1552-1629). As part of his map of Wiltshire, he created one of the most widely reproduced images of the stone circle. He first published his maps, *The Theatre of the Empire of Great Britain*, in 1612. The book contained 67 painstakingly drawn maps of the counties of England, Scotland, Ireland and Wales. Speed's maps are works of art, featuring scenes from notable local events as well as three-dimensional drawings of important features.

Speed began life as a tailor, but thanks to rich patron, Sir Fulke Greville, he was able to study and became a historian, publishing his *History of Great Britain* in 1600. He felt a lively atlas was needed to complement it, and set to work on the project he is remembered for today. In 1595, he published his first map, which was a four-sheet recreation of Canaan in Biblical times. He followed it with one of the Holy Land. His Wiltshire map, as well as its striking view of Stonehenge, features a detailed plan of the city of Salisbury, and a text panel stating that Stonehenge was built by 'Ambrosianus, King of the Brittaines'.

GETTING THE LEY OF THE LAND

Numerous ley lines are supposed to converge on or pass by Stonehenge. Here are the sites that lie on the ley line known as The Old Sarum Ley, going from south to north.

Clearbury Ring • Durrington Down Barrow
Frankenbury Camp hill fort • Old Sarum hill fort (crosses Stonehenge Ley) • Salisbury Cathedral spire • Stonehenge cursus • Stonehenge ditch

SARSEN SLEDS

Back in 1901, William Gowland proposed a solution to the mystery of how the great Sarsen stones were moved from Marlborough Downs into their current position, which has been widely accepted ever since.

His method involved levering the stone from its environment and putting timber supports under it as it was raised. When as much as possible had been levered up, a massive, wooden sled-like structure would be pushed underneath as close as possible, and the supports slowly removed until the stone slid back onto it. Large teams of men then dragged the sled across country, using a series of wooden logs as rollers. He based his method on what we know of the moving of huge stones in Ancient Egypt, and much more recent building work involving large stones in Japan. It is still considered the most likely way in which the heaviest stones, weighing perhaps 50 tonnes, reached the henge.

WILLIAM STUKELEY (1687-1765)

William Stukeley, doctor and then Reverend, not only produced one of the first serious studies of Stonehenge and Avebury, he also started the fashion in the eighteenth century for Druidism.

Born in Lincolnshire in 1687, he studied at Cambridge and then St Thomas's Hospital, London. He would eventually become a Fellow of the Royal College of Physicians in 1720 after returning to London in 1717, where he also joined the Royal Society. In 1718, he was happy to accept the post of first secretary of the Society of Antiquaries of London (which he himself had helped to establish), under whose auspices he was able to excavate at both Stonehenge and Avebury during breaks from his other careers. In 1721, he became a convert to freemasonry, joining the Grand Lodge that had just been set up in London, and writing lengthily on the subject. Around 1729 or 1730 he had something of a religious epiphany, and in 1730 was ordained in the Church of England.

While a student at Cambridge, Stukeley had started to sketch architectural features and scenes. He published the *Itinerarium Curiosum* in 1724, hoping to preserve data about antiquities which were being destroyed in the name of modernisation.

In 1740, he published a volume on Stonehenge, and followed that in 1743 with one on Avebury. He noted the solar alignment of Stonehenge, and stated that the monumental stones were prehistoric in origin, and built by the Druids. *Abury, A Temple of the British Druids with Some Others, Described, is a more particular account of the first and patriarchal religion; and of the peopling the British Islands*, to give it its full title, begins: 'Of the origin of Druid or patriarchal temples, with publick religion and celebration of the Sabbath. They were made of rude stones set upright in the ground, round in form, and open. In hot countries, groves were planted about them. Abraham practised it, and from him our Druids.'

Stukeley believed Anglican Christianity was descended from Druidism, and he was careful to emphasise that Druids worshipped the one true God. He investigated Neolithic structures around the country with a passion, looking for more Druid temples. Despite creating a huge prehistorical red herring by connecting Stonehenge and the Druids, he did much important work. As well as noting its alignment with the solstices, he was one of the first to consider monuments in their landscape. He drew accurate topographical views of the surrounding area.

Apart from informing his parishioners that Druids were the fathers of the Church of England, Stukeley had a few other eccentric interests. He wrote music for the flute, was a prolific essayist, composing treatises on gout, earthquakes and Robin Hood, as well as penning a life of his friend, Sir Isaac Newton.

*The peculiar weather on Salisbury plain baffled
even the hardiest meteorologists*

DURRINGTON WALLS

Durrington Walls is the largest henge in the Stonehenge area, a huge earthwork enclosure over 470 metres across with a massive ditch over six metres deep and 13 metres wide. It lies on the sloping bank of the River Avon to the north-east of Stonehenge and has two main entrances, one of which points down towards the river.

Large-scale excavations in 1966 and 1968 when the road through the henge was straightened revealed the remains of two large timber circles of oak posts, the largest 23 metres in diameter. Whether these are the remains of circles of free-standing posts or of roofed timber buildings is uncertain. Finds of large quantities of decorated pottery, known as 'Grooved Ware' and of animal bones, particularly pig bones, suggest that these circles were places where feasting took place, perhaps at midwinter.

More recent excavations have discovered a ceremonial roadway or avenue leading down towards the river and the remains of small square houses, the first of this period to have been found in the Stonehenge area.

Durrington was built and used over many centuries, but was a flourishing centre at the same time that Stonehenge was being rebuilt in stone, around 2,500 to 2,300 BC.

YOU'RE MY INSPIRATION

Over the centuries the sight of Stonehenge has inspired many famous people to pen poetry celebrating the stones. Here are just a few:

WH Auden • William Blake • William Empson
Ann Finch, Countess of Winchilsea
Thomas Hardy • Siegfried Sassoon
Sir Philip Sidney • JRR Tolkien
Thomas Wharton • William Wordsworth

ANGELS IN THE ANGLES

If you accept the fact that the builders of Stonehenge were sun worshippers, or astronomers, who sited it precisely, you should be able to work out when it was built by looking at the position in which the sun was in relation to the stones in any given year (which shifts fractionally over centuries as the Earth tilts on its axis). By finding the perfect match between orientation and midsummer sunrise, you should find the age of the building.

That was what Egyptologist William Flinders Petrie thought, anyway. Stonehenge is built on an axis that follows the midwinter sunset/midsummer sunrise, the avenue leading from it follows that line, and it is aligned towards the midsummer sunrise, rather than the midwinter sunset,

because the horseshoe of trilithons points that way. So far, so good.

Flinders Petrie's first problem was that half the sighting mechanism was missing – in Flinders Petrie's time, the Great Trilithon leaned dramatically, and now only one of its uprights is standing, so it was impossible for him, and us, to accurately line it up with the gap between stones 1 and 30. The second was in working out what the Ancient Britons counted as sunrise. Was it the first halo of light on the horizon, or the first beams from the top of the sun's disc? Did the whole sun have to be visible? Flinders Petrie made some educated guesses and came up with a very wrong date of 730 AD – it wasn't just the guestimates involved, he was also very bad at maths.

QUOTE UNQUOTE

His functions, simply stated, were to act as adviser to kings and rulers, as judge, as teacher, and as an authority in matters of worship and ceremony... The classical texts never refer to them as priests, but as philosophers.
Philip Carr-Gomm, author, writing in *The Druid Tradition*

What is a henge?
a) A place where sacrifices took place in prehistoric times
b) A place where people were executed by hanging
c) Another name for a circle of standing stones
d) A circular bank with a ditch inside it
Answer on page 153.

BEST OF BRITISH

Seahenge, Holme-next-the-Sea, Norfolk

A few miles from King's Lynn lies one of the most extraordinary ancient monuments you'll ever 'see'. In fact, if you visit the beach at Holme-next-the-Sea you won't see what was discovered there in 1999 – the worn remains of 55 huge oak posts surrounding a two-and-a-half-tonne oak tree trunk embedded, upside down, in the sand. Photographs from 1999 show a haunting landscape with the huge roots of the oak blasting out towards the sky, and the stumps of the original henge just peeking from the water. The posts would originally have completely enclosed the trunk in a wooden wall, similar to the 'palisade enclosures' thought to have stood near Avebury.

Immersion in the sea saved parts of the Seahenge palisade, and a shifting of the sands has uncovered them after probably being buried for centuries. The wood is so well preserved that the henge can be dated precisely by the rings in the tree trunks to 2,049 BC. When Seahenge was first spotted, the beach surrounding it was swiftly designated a Site of Special Scientific Interest, and English Heritage stepped in to assess how best to preserve such a difficult area – part submerged, and set on shifting sands, in danger of being overwhelmed by visitors excited by the new find, and exposed to violent storms.

In the end, although controversial, English Heritage opted for an exhaustive survey of the site before removing the central trunk and 55 posts to the Flag Fen Archaeological Centre, near Peterborough. The centre specialises in the study of prehistoric timber. There, the posts are stored in water tanks and analysis has discovered the marks of 51 separate metal tools on them, the earliest evidence of the use of such tools in Britain.

Some people wish for the site's restoration; others think that time and tide should have been left to do its work. Tidal erosion is slowly revealing the salt marsh landscape our distant ancestors would have walked upon, as it peels back the layers of peat.

GETTING THE LEY OF THE LAND II

Numerous ley lines are supposed to converge on or pass by Stonehenge. Here are the sites that lie on the 22-mile south-west north-east ley line, known as The Stonehenge Ley.

Castle Ditches Hill Fort
Cow Down Tumuli
Dew Pond • Grovely Castle
Silbury Camp Hill Fort
Stonehenge approach avenue
Stonehenge Bell Barrow, Normanton Down

DEATH WISHES

At the midnight then sent the chamber-knights six of their men to Appas's inn; they weened to find him, and bring him to the king. Then was he flown, and the fiends him carried! The men came back where the king dwelt, and made known in the chamber of Appas's departure. Then might men see sorrow enow be! Knights fell down, and yearned their deaths; there was mickle lamentation and heart-groaning, there was many a piteous speech, there was yell of men! They leapt to the bed, and beheld the king; the yet he lay in slumber, and in great sweat. The knights with weeping awakened the king, and they called to him with mild voice: 'Lord, how is it with thee? how is thy harm? For now is our leech departed without leave, gone out of court, and left us as wretches.' The king gave them answer: 'I am all over swollen, and there is no other hap, now anon I shall be dead. And I bid forth-right, ye who are my knights, that ye greet Uther, who is my own brother, and bid him hold my land in his sway. God himself through all things let him be a good king! And bid him be keen, and always deem right, as a father to the poor folk, to the destitute for comfort; – then may he hold the land in power. And now to-day, when I be dead, take ye all one counsel, and cause me to be brought Tight to Stonehenge, where lie much of my kindred, by the Saxons killed. And send for bishops, and book-learned men; my gold and silver distribute for my soul, and lay me at the east end, in Stonehenge.' There was no other hap – there was the king dead! And all so his men did as the king directed. Uther was in Wales, and hereof was nothing ware, never through any art hereof nothing wist; nevertheless he had with him the prophet Merlin, he proceeded towards the army that was come to the land.

Wace Layamon,
Arthurian Chronicles, 1912

SPOOKY STONEHENGE

The haunted barrow

The West Kennett Long Barrow stands out as one of the best-preserved Neolithic tombs in the country, as well as the only one that's supposed to be haunted. It's close to Avebury and its stone circle, as well as Silbury Hill. Inside the barrow, parts of almost 50 different skeletons have been found, along with one single complete skeleton – some believe bones were taken at different intervals for use in ceremonies. In the late seventeenth century, a local doctor dug up bones from the barrow, ground them up and used them in medicines.

Reports of the West Kennett haunting seem, for the most part, to be quite ancient. The ghostly figure of a priest is seen entering the barrow on Midsummer's Day, at sunrise. His companion is a white dog with red ears, which folklorists interpret as a symbol of the 'other world' of Faerie (red ears being traditional among fairy folk, and not, it must be said, common on earthly white dogs) or a shuck, a kind of malevolent ghost dog, more usually black with fiery red eyes, who appears in legends throughout the British Isles, often as a symbol of impending death.

QUOTE UNQUOTE

'You won't see Stonehenge every day, young man,' said the custodian, a little piqued.
'It's only an old beach,' said the small boy, with extreme conviction.
'It's rocks like the seaside. And there isnt no sea.'
HG Wells, author, writing in *The Secret Places of the Heart*

SPEED'S LOST STONEHENGE

Little is known about the career of dramatist and academician John Speed, as he was writing just before the Puritans closed the theatres and banned dramatic presentations as 'ungodly'. But we do know he wrote a pastoral play entitled *Stonehenge* in the 1630s. Indeed, his *Stonehenge* was far advanced enough in 1634 for him to mention it to a contemporary, who obligingly made a note of the conversation, describing it as 'A Play of Pastroall', and in 1636 it was performed at Cambridge before Dr Richard Baylie, then president of the university, shortly after he had returned from being installed as Dean of Salisbury. Since we know it was being written, or even finished in 1634 it's unlikely the drama was written for the occasion, but it was clearly a lucky coincidence that Salisbury was close to Stonehenge. A contemporary source notes: 'The said Pastoral is not printed, but goes about in MS from hand to hand', which perhaps explains why it is now lost.

Returning from Stonehenge, the Simms family agreed that there was nothing in all that 'magical ley lines' nonsense

HOW DID THE BUILDING MATERIALS GET THERE?

Throughout the ages a number of scientific, pseudo-scientific and, frankly, barmy ideas have been put forward to explain how the various types of stone from which Stonehenge was constructed came from and how they were transported to the site.

1. Magical machines
2. Popped up in a volcanic eruption
3. Deposited by melting glaciers
4. Solids thrown up when the molten earth first began to rotate
5. Fallen from space
6. Rolled on poles
8. Carried by giants

One of the most famous paintings of Stonehenge was done by Lucas de Heere, a Protestant refugee from Ghent. He fled his homeland in 1567 when the Duke of Alva's inquisition arrived in the Netherlands, and didn't return until 1576. In those eight years he not only continued to paint, but between 1573 and 1575 also wrote an early guidebook for fellow Netherlanders arriving in Great Britain, which circulated in London as a manuscript.

Corte Beschryvinghe van England, Scotland ende Irland covered the peculiarities of British taste, customs, costume and history, as well as some of the more notable sights. Perhaps because of his artist's eye, his description of the henge is particularly accurate: 'These mentioned stones are massive [and] undressed, from hard coarse material, of grey colour. They are generally about 18 or 20 feet high and about 8 feet wide over all four sides [for they are square]. They stand two by two, each couple having one stone across, like a gallows, which stone has two mortises catching two stone tenons of the two upright stones.' De Heere has clearly paid attention, and goes on to say how he thinks the stones would have looked before they began to fall, the width of the circle, etc. He then goes a little astray remarking: 'One finds here-about many small hillocks of monticules, under which are sometimes found giant's bones (of which I possess one from which it can easily be perceived that the giant was as much as 12 feet tall…)'.

De Heere became the first artist to draw Stonehenge accurately from life – a watercolour appears on the one surviving copy of his guide, written in his own hand. He chose a raised perspective so the arrangement of the stones could be seen more easily, and demonstrated the scale by including a knight in armour and a man standing beside the nearest stone, although he did move the ditch in rather close to the stones. He does misplace some stones (stone 56, for example, the leaning trilithon upright), and omit some fallen ones, but the picture is still recognisable to us today, with its three central trilithons and scattered Sarsen uprights, only those on the left providing an uninterrupted run of lintels.

Soon afterwards, another popular image of Stonehenge was drawn, this time by William Smith, a royal herald, and included in his 1588 manuscript, *A Particular Description of England*. Smith's picture is from the north-west side. Instead of a knight, he has several groups of strollers, and de Heere's measuring man at the front has become a vandal scrawling graffiti. Some of Smith's lintels have now turned into pillars balanced across the uprights like giant sticks of rock.

WHILE YOU'RE IN THE AREA WHY NOT VISIT...

Wilton House

You may be tempted by Wilton House's Tudor kitchen, Victorian laundry and kids' adventure playground, but anyone with any sense visits Wilton House for one reason and one reason alone: to see the magnificent Inigo Jones Staterooms and, of course, their contents. The Double Cube Room, in particular, reckoned to be the finest seventeenth-century stateroom in England, was specially built to showcase family portraits by Van Eyke. These wonderful pictures represent the largest collection of Van Eykes still being shown in their original setting in the world, and are worth the price of admission. The Earl of Pembroke (whose ancestor, you'll remember, was fond of forestry enclosure – see page 11) maintains the house and 20 acres of gardens in the grand style that they were originally conceived. The house itself, though, was first used as a nunnery in the ninth century.

THE GENTEEL ROUGH GUIDE

About 1 1/2 M. to the W. lies 'Stonehenge' (called by the Saxons Stanhengest i.e. 'hanging stones', formerly Choir Gaur or Côr Gawr, Giant's Circle or temple), the most imposing megalithic monument in Britain, now surrounded by a barbed-wire fence (adm. 1s.) When complete it seems to have consisted of two concentric circles, enclosing two ellipses. Of the outer circle, about 100ft in diameter, 16 stones are still standing, and 5 of the huge flat cap-stones remain in position. The larger circle and ellipse are formed of 'Sarsen' sandstone; the others (perhaps earlier in date) are of 'blue-stone', a kind of granite. The sacred road leading to the circles can be traced by its banks of earth. The isolated stone at some distance from the rest is known as the 'Friar's heel'. The origin and purpose of Stonehenge are still unknown. 'It has been attributed,' says Chambers's Encyclopedia, 'to the Phoenicians, the Belgae, the Druids, the Saxons and the Danes'. It has been called a temple of the sun, and of serpent worship, a shrine of Buddha, a planetarium, a gigantic swallow on which defeated English leaders were solemnly hung in honour of Woden, a Gilgal where the national army met and leaders were buried, and a calendar in stone for the measurement of the solar year.

Now it is most generally classed as a sepulchral stone circle, perhaps exceptionally developed under some religious influence, and is usually connected with the 'round barrows' or bowl-shaped burial tumuli of the 3rd cent BC which lie around in hundreds.

JF Muirhead,
Baedeker Great Britain, 1910
(seventh edition)

WILTSHIRE WHITE HORSES

Wiltshire is dotted with hill carvings, particularly white horses, some of which are thought to date back to the ninth century. However, the dates are often muddled because it's hard to distinguish restoration in the eighteenth and nineteenth centuries from actually carving them out of the hillside. Here are a dozen places to see the magnificent white horses in the country.

Westbury (restored in 1778, thought to be much older)

Oldbury (1780)

Pewsey (1785)

Marlborough (1804, restored late nineteenth century)

Alton Barnes (1812)

Hackpen (1838)

Devizes (1845)

Broad Town (1863)

Ham Hill (1860s)

Pewsey (1937, a very late entry!)

ANTIQUARIAN ASSUMPTIONS

The assumptions that early commentators made about Stonehenge may sound ludicrous to us now, but we must look at them in a wider context. Several widely accepted ideas rather hamstrung any scholar investigating ancient monuments.

For a start, people like John Aubrey and William Stukeley had no idea about ages of human development. For them, there was no Stone Age or Iron Age. Darwin hadn't yet written about determinism and it was widely accepted that God had created the Earth in seven days around five and a half thousand years ago. Even the more radical thinkers among the scientific community, who attempted to date the Earth using physical evidence, got it wrong by billions of years. So every civilisation, fossil and remain had to be fitted into a small timespan, explaining some of the more inaccurate dating that went on.

Furthermore, when presented with different styles of tools from various digs, antiquarians came to the conclusion that their ancestors had employed different tools according to their rank in life. Thus the rich men had bronze tools, the artisans used iron, and the poor stone. The existence of different strata with different remains at different depths completely escaped them, and it wasn't until as late as the 1850s that the notion of different ages of man was understood.

PLAYING FAVOURITES

In 1620, he was employed in a manner very unworthy of his genius. King James set him upon discovering, that is, guessing who were the founders of Stonehenge. His ideas were all romanized; consequently, his partiality to his favourite people, which ought rather to have prevented him from charging them with that mass of barbarous clumsiness, made him conclude it a Roman temple. It is remarkable, that whoever has treated of that monument, has bestowed it on whatever class of antiquity he was peculiarly fond of; and there is not a heap of stones in these northern countries, from which nothing can be proved, but has been made to depose in favour of some of these fantastic hypotheses. Where there was so much room for visions, the Phoenicians could not avoid coming in for their share of the foundation; and for Mr. Toland's part, he discovered a little Stonehenge in Ireland, built by the Druidess Gealcopa, (who does not know the Druidess Gealcopa?) who lived at Inisioen, in the county of Donegal.

Horace Walpole and Ralph N Wornum,
Anecdotes of Painting in England:
With Some Account of the Principal Artists Vol 2, **1888**
(Quite what this has to do with painting in England is anyone's guess.)

THE RIVERSIDE PROJECT

Mike Parker Pearson, Senior Lecturer at the Department of Archaeology and Prehistory at Sheffield University, began a project a few years ago designed to examine Stonehenge as part of a wider landscape in an attempt to understand its function over many centuries. The Riverside Project, as it has become known, came about following fieldwork in Madagascar where Pearson worked with local Malagasy archaeologist Ramilisonina. In Madagascar great stone and timber structures were being built by primitive peoples until comparatively recently.

Pearson, a specialist in death and burials, was inspired when his colleague Ramilisonina pointed out that to wonder why a large group of living Neolithic people gathered to build Stonehenge was to miss the point entirely because it was clearly built for the ancestors, eternal and enduring, just like the stone itself. Ramilisonina also pointed out that the echoing of the more permanent stone monoliths with wooden posts could have been representative of the ancestors and the living.

Pearson's excavations focus on the idea of Stonehenge as part of a riverside funery procession route, along the river Avon, up the avenue, and to the monument itself, and also include Woodhenge and Durrington Walls.

FAMOUS DRUIDS

Nowadays, Druidic orders can't claim many famous members – William Roache, who plays Ken Barlow on *Coronation Street,* is probably the world's most famous Druid at the moment – but over the years, quite a selection of famous names have been involved in Druidism. Some are well known, while others are impossible to prove or disprove. Modern Druidism also has the habit of awarding Druid status to people they think are worthy of it, willy-nilly, which is why Rowan Williams, the Archbishop of Canterbury, was recently declared a Druid.

Ludwig van Beethoven, composer
William Blake, poet and visionary
William Burroughs, visionary and writer
Rachel Carson, environmental activist
Winston Churchill, Prime Minister
Nicolaus Copernicus, astronomer
Scott Cunningham, Wiccan writer
Salvador Dali, artist and, er, visionary
Dion Fortune, occult author
Benjamin Franklin, politician and freethinker
Galileo Galilei, astronomer
Gerald Gardner, witch
Johannes Kepler, astronomer
S Macgregor Mathers, occultist
Wolfgang Amadeus Mozart, composer
John Muir, Victorian travel writer
Albert Schweitzer, peace activist
Oscar Wilde, wit
Frank Lloyd Wright, architect
William Butler Yeats, poet

RESULTS ORIENTATED

Professor William Gowland (a mining specialist rather than an archaeologist) successfully straightened stone 56 in 1901, as a result of the safety inspection undertaken following the great gale of 1900. Despite the fact that he only investigated the area immediately around the stone, he was also able to record a wealth of new information about Stonehenge including:

1. The methods used to dig the stone holes
2. How the Sarsen stones were trimmed and shaped
3. How the Sarsen stones were erected
4. Proof that the bluestones and Sarsens were of similar date
5. Proof that the bluestones in the inner horseshoe must have been raised after the trilithons

John Wood the Elder (1704-1754) will chiefly be remembered as the architect who mapped out the Georgian city of Bath and built many of its landmark buildings. Locally born, and the son of a builder, Wood began his career as an architect early and by the age of 17 was so far advanced as to build speculative houses in London to take advantage of the building boom in London following the 1713 treaty of Utrecht. Although it almost led to his bankruptcy, in the end he was successful and went on to a 30-year career in which each building he produced seemed to outshine the previous. When he died, in 1754, work had just begun on Bath's famous Circus.

What made Wood an outstanding architect was his grasp of town planning and his desire to create a truly British kind of architecture. He designed buildings grouped to provide magnificent vistas, and planned the first crescent-shaped lines of terraced houses built in England. Most grand buildings at the time modelled their facades on the ideals of ancient Greece and Rome, but Wood drew on wider sources, believing he was creating an order of architecture that reflected the intrinsic Britishness of its origins.

While on one hand a man of reason, Wood was also a keen Freemason, a student of ancient lore – with particular interest in the ancient British king Bladud who was supposed to have been the first person to recognise the healing powers of the hot springs at Bath – and a Druid-fancier. In 1740, he made an extremely well-annotated survey of Stonehenge which would be referred to for decades to come, the first to carefully record which stones were standing, leaning, fallen or lying on top of each other.

Wood used the esoteric interest to design buildings whose proportions and mathematical relationships echoed not those of the Parthenon, but of Stonehenge itself. Bath Circus has the same diameter as Stonehenge, and is decorated with emblems inspired by Druidism and Freemasonry. It was finished by his son, John Wood Jr.

QUOTE UNQUOTE

'It looks,' Sir Richmond said, 'as though some old giantess had left a discarded set of teeth on the hillside.' Far more impressive than Stonehenge itself were the barrows that capped the neighbouring crests.
HG Wells, author, writing in *The Secret Places of the Heart*

Old Sarum Castle

About 3,000 years before the birth of Christ, Neolithic man was living at Old Sarum, no doubt attracted by its location on top of a hill. During the Iron Age, from about 500 BC onwards, settlers built a large hill fort which could be used as a place of safety during times of threat, but also as a central marketplace and meeting place. The Romans put it to good use when they were trying to subdue the tribes of Wessex around 60 AD, and after them the Saxons moved in, renaming Old Sarum *Searobyrg* and basing the centre of one of their kingdoms there.

After the Norman conquest, William I inherited the fort from the last Saxon king and built a motte and bailey castle there in 1069, which he visited a year later. By 1075, the first cathedral on the site was built, then rebuilt in 1120, when Old Sarum was the seat of the local bishop.

However, in the early thirteenth century, the town's fortunes began to decline. The bishop decamped to nearby Salisbury and, by the early sixteenth century, the castle was considered so primitive and ill-favoured that Henry VII gave it to Thomas Compton to pull down for building materials. What you see now looks much more like the original hill fort, overgrown with green, with few signs of its medieval heyday showing.

CAMBRY AND CARNAC

Among the most zealous (and diffident) writers on ancient monuments was a theorist from the nineteenth century, Jacques de Cambry. In his *Monuments Celtiques*, which was dedicated to Napoleon, de Cambry's revolutionary fervour led him to declare that not only were the Gauls, Celts and Franks all the same people, but they were also the original civilisation from which all other great civilisations copied. In short, when Napoleon travelled to Egypt and claimed the pyramids for France he was only reclaiming what really belonged to French culture in the first place!

De Cambry's book started off about 'the oldest, greatest monument' at Carnac, then contained a lengthy attack on French scholarship for ignoring the claims of Breton culture as established by the Celtic Druids, unlike the English who made so much of Stonehenge. Egyptians or other foreigners didn't come to Carnac to erect the stones, it was the locals who went off and scattered the knowledge to build monuments, such as Stonehenge, across the globe – hence the congruency scholars had noted in their designs, measurements or locations. Furthermore, the hated English had, in fact, copied not just their monuments, but also their artistic, architectural, legal and political systems from the ancient French.

In the 1950s, Alexander Thom, a professor of mechanical engineering at Oxford, began considering if the motivation of stone circle builders, as a whole, had been to create astronomical tools. Why, Thom asked himself, if Neolithic man had the skill to create a complex astronomical observatory or even a primitive computer like Stonehenge, did he not build other observatories that would demonstrate the degree of precision at Stonehenge?

Thom began examining stone circles in Britain and France, and through careful measurement began to see that Neolithic man not only created many ways of observing the motions of the sun and moon, but also demonstrated a high level of skill when it came to building measurements and geometry by using a megalithic yard of 2.72 feet, a megalithic fathom of 5.44 feet and also a small megalithic inch. He began to see that what seemed to be rough stone circles, had originally been laid out to sophisticated plans that included ovals and egg shapes.

Thom concentrated his studies on less well known earthworks and circles, and built up a vast body of evidence, which he started publishing in 1954. When he was finally persuaded to examine Stonehenge in 1973, he found it displayed a similar awareness of astronomy, geometry and measurement that the other buildings he'd looked at had – the Sarsen circle fitted with his system of measurement, and its planning showed an advanced knowledge of geometry. He disagreed with the lunar alignments, saying the sight lines were too short to have been useful to early astronomers. He did identify other lunar lines of sight and co-related them with earthworks on the horizon.

Thom's son, Archibald Thom made further advances when he analysed markings on a gold plaque found in a barrow nearby. He suggested these were related to recording a solar and lunar calendar from observations made at Stonehenge. Previously, supporters of the astronomical theory had failed to discover any evidence of records being kept. Surely a major part of the point of building such a gigantic structure?

The theory gained further support with the examination of the chambered tomb found at Newgrange in Ireland, where its function as a solar observatory aligned to the midwinter sunrise depended on two-dimensional lines of sight and on a slope to the floor of the chamber from which observation would have had to be made. Without the slope, it just would not work. This suggests the orientation and placement of objects can't have been accidental, and points to developed Neolithic scientific thought – and a body of people who has sufficient power and patience to have built such observatories and then used them for many years to obtain results.

A handful of archaeologists wondered if a class of scientists, distinct from the general populace, rather like shamen or the later Druids, had existed. If so, had they at one time or another been based at nearby Durrington Walls, a henge located near Stonehenge which demonstrated signs of occupation by a large group judging from the animal bones and other remains that have been dug up there?

However compelling the theory was, later discoveries began to undermine its foundations, at least in relation to Stonehenge. Some of the distant earthworks Thom thought were markers on the horizon turned out to date back no further than the English Civil War. And a small hump known as Peter's Mound was, in fact, a rubbish tip from the twentieth century which happened to align perfectly from Stonehenge with the prehistoric midsummer sunrise. Scientists then began to test the geometrical hypotheses. They came up with simpler explanations for the number of carefully aligned circles Thom found, as well as pointing out that the megalithic yard was sufficiently close to a human pace, a measurement often used in laying out early buildings.

CASTING THE RUNES

What exactly is a megalith?
a) Two large standing stones with another one balanced across the top?
b) A big stone
c) A stone that has been shaped or carved by prehistoric man?
d) A blue stone
Answer on page 153.

STICKING TO HIS GUNS

Sir Edmund Antrobus complained that people were always advising (or telling him) what he must do to Stonehenge. In the end, he had the last laugh. Modern archaeologists are delighted that he left the site much as he found it, apart from a few stout timber bracers. Here are a few of the schemes he resisted:

1. Digging a moat around the monument, presumably to keep people out
2. Digging a ha-ha to limit access to the stones
3. Building a cottage beside it to house a policeman to watch over the stones, day and night
4. Any excavation work, except for one request from a Captain Beamish around 1839
5. The lifting of fallen stones or cementing of leaning ones
6. A fence made of iron railings all the way around the monument, which would have been a huge undertaking and completely spoiled the view

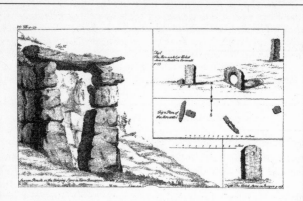

'Antiquities of Cornwall', W Borlase, 1769

RUDE CYCLOPEAN ARCHITECTURE

This much must be said about the New Stone people: they had a great skill in a form of rude Cyclopean architecture, since it was to their labours that we owe such remarkable megalithic edifices as Stonehenge and Avebury, at least so we now think. They were also the constructors of immense earthen fortresses, like that at Maiden Castle between Weymouth and Dorchester (Dorset), which afford evidence as to their numbers and perseverance since they were unprovided with any but the most primitive kind of tools. They constructed a rude but useful kind of pottery of a purely hand-made character, for the potter's wheel had yet to make its appearance in Britain. They could spin and weave; they grew a poor kind of corn as well as flax; they kept cattle and pigs and had a domesticated dog. The mammoth, the cave-bear, the reindeer, all the other strange wild beasts which the men of the Old Stone Age had encountered, had gone, but there were still wolves, wild boars and cats, beavers and deer – all, but the last, now extinct in the country – as well as herds of the great white cattle which remain with us, but only in the shape of a few very carefully tended herds in close captivity. In addition, there were, of course, the various wild animals with which we are familiar to-day.

Bertram CA Windle, *The Romans In Britain,* **1923**

No one who has studied phallic and solar worship in the East could make any mistake as to the purport of the shrine at Stonehenge… yet the indelicacy of the whole subject often so shocks the ordinary reader, that, in spite of facts, he cannot grant what he thinks shows so much debasement of the religious mind; facts are facts, however, and it only remains for us to account for them.

James George Roche Forlong, writing in *Cyclopaedia of Religions*

MEGALITHS DU MONDE

Waitapu Stone Circle, New Zealand

Calling Waitapu a stone circle is a tad misleading. More accurately, it is a huge scattering of stones, almost certainly man-made, which kinda-sorta fits into a plan of a double, interlinked stone circle and kinda-sorta aligns with various heavenly bodies if you squint and tilt your head a bit. Unfortunately, of the 600 stones on Maunganui Bluff in the Waitapu valley, none are left standing, having supposedly been knocked down by Maori warriors some 400 years ago. Current interpretations of the confused layout rely on the fact that the Maoris knocked them over, but didn't move them around.

Astronomers, astroarchaeologists, historians and geologists are at loggerheads over evidence that has been recently published about New Zealand's Celtic civilisations, and the Waitapu circle is at the centre of this controversy. The accepted version has the Maoris as the original inhabitants of New Zealand, arriving from Polynesia somewhere around 1,250 AD to 1,350 AD, and some believe that the New Zealand Department of Conservation has been suppressing evidence of the existence of a pre-Polynesian civilisation some five millennia older for years, noting that an archaeological report into the possible ruins of an ancient 'stacked' city in Waipoua Forest has been suppressed for 75 years.

The original hornets' nest was stirred up by Martin Doutré in his book *Ancient Celtic New Zealand*, which was first published in 1999. Not only did he identify the scattered stones of Waitapu as an ancient astronomical observatory, but he also found evidence of many other sites whose placement was linked to the stars, all over the surrounding Aranga district. Since then, largely amateur astroarchaeologists have been reporting evidence of canals for irrigation, landscape reshaping, Neolithic villages, burial sites and thousands of cairns. So many that New Zealand may soon trump Britain as the most densely 'stoned' country in the world.

SEVEN WONDERS OF GREAT BRITAIN

In 2002, the Yellow Pages telephone directory asked 2,500 adults from across the country to name their local 'Seven Wonders'. Stonehenge came second, behind the Houses of Parliament. In a similar exercise, teenagers voted Alton Towers our most impressive achievement, but they still regarded Stonehenge as third best.

Houses of Parliament and Big Ben

Stonehenge • Windsor Castle

Eden Project • York Minster

Hadrian's Wall • London Eye

SPOOKY STONEHENGE

The Warminster thing

On Christmas Eve 1964, people around Warminster, which is 15 miles west of Stonehenge, heard an incredible high-pitched whine which ended up incapacitating several of them. Lights in the sky soon followed. This was the first of many sightings of what local journalist Arthur Shuttlewood christened 'the Warminster thing'. Sometimes people saw discs, sometimes cigar shapes, or fiery balls, and newspaper reports at the time suggested that around 800 of Warminster's 11,000 inhabitants had experienced a close encounter of some kind – an extraordinarily high percentage.

Warminster's close proximity to the military bases on Salisbury Plain have led some people to dismiss these phenomena as the result of seeing experimental military aircraft. And Arthur Shuttlewood's zealous promotion of the area as somewhere you were almost guaranteed to see a mystery object – he claimed at various times to have had hundreds of encounters each year, and to have seen a saucer land – caused him to come into conflict with many other UFO researchers. In 1968, he reported seeing a craft that looked like a circle of fire over Stonehenge which, when he approached it, shot straight up into the sky.

For years following the first manifestations, UFOlogists and sightseers would gather on Cradle and Cley Hills to look and listen for the unusual piercing noises and their accompanying lights – 10,000 visitors flooded the area for the August Bank Holiday in 1965. And in one bumper year, up to 1,000 unexplained sightings were recorded. But whatever was going on in Warminster in the 1960s and 1970s, nowadays sightings have pretty much dried up, and interest has refocused on alien contact and abductions, rather than colourful fly-bys, no matter how frequent.

BEST BOOKS

Of all the thousands of books available, we found these to be both readable and informative – a rare combination.

Stonehenge Complete, Christopher Chippindale
(Thames and Hudson)

Stonehenge, A History in Photographs, Julian Richards
(English Heritage)

Standing Stones: Carnac, Stonehenge and the World of Megaliths, Jean-Pierre Mohem
(Thames and Hudson)

Beyond Stonehenge, Gerald S Hawkins
(Hubert Allen & Associates)

The Druids, Peter Berresford Ellis (Constable)

The Lost Gods of England, Brian Branston (Constable)

Stonehenge: Celebration and Subversion, Andy Worthington
(Alternative Albion)

And just for fun:

Stonehenge, Robin Heath (Wooden Books)

The Amazing Pop-Up Stonehenge, Julian Richards
(English Heritage)

WHILE YOU'RE IN THE AREA WHY NOT VISIT...

Wilton Windmill

It's amazing to consider how many thousands of windmills once turned in Great Britain, and how many are now gone. Every small village had one – I spent my adolescence in a wind-whipped house built where the village windmill once stood. Nowadays, working windmills are hard to find, which is why it's worth stopping off at the Wilton Windmill, near Marlborough, for a look at how they used to produce flour 150 years ago. The mill stands high on a chalk ridge, and is visible for miles around, which is just as well as the roads are twisty. By night it's a local landmark, standing in floodlit splendour overlooking the nearby villages of Great Bedwyn and Burbage. It's a working mill, fully restored, and you can tour the interior on Sundays between Easter and September (and buy some quality stoneground flour, of course).

Number of spaces for cars in the Stonehenge visitors' car park 123

QUOTE UNQUOTE

Geoffrey [of Monmouth]'s claim that the stones originally came from Africa may have been prompted by the Roman olive presses of North Africa, which are of trilithon shape and which up to the nineteenth century were believed to be prehistoric monuments.
Jennifer Westwood, author

CASTING THE RUNES

What is the term for cutting giant chalk figures into hillsides?
a) Hippotomy
b) Leuccipotomy
c) Homogigantry
d) Gigantotomy
Answer on page 153.

WHAT IS SARSEN?

One of the reasons Stonehenge has survived so well is that the major uprights are made from Sarsen stone, a kind of sandstone that is particularly hard and durable. It is up to seven times harder than granite, for instance. Sarsen – the name derives from Saracen, but the boulders were also known as 'greywether' – is naturally found in large blocks. It was formed when sand was compressed on the seabed among chalk beds. Following up to 70 million years of pressure, the sand forms into irregular blocks which, because of the strata of the chalk, tend to be quite rectangular.

There are major Sarsen deposits at nearby Marlborough, and others scattered around southern England. Although it is assumed that the builders of Stonehenge got their Sarsens from the Marlborough area, there is no actual proof that this is so, and the Sarsens that remain in the area are far smaller than those found at Stonehenge.

However, it's very possible that all the larger stones have been used up, chiefly for posts, pillars and road surfacing. Although ideal for builders interested in working at gigantic scale, anyone wanting more control over the stone faces problems. Medieval builders tended to avoid Sarsen for this very reason and it wasn't until the nineteenth century that a method was devised for easily splitting the huge slabs. Before that, stone masons had to settle for just smashing them into irregular, rough boulders, then cementing them together as best they could.

LOCKYER'S LEYS

A few years after William Flinders Petrie's attempt to date Stonehenge precisely, celebrated astronomer Sir Norman Lockyer decided to have a go. He arrived at a slightly more accurate date (1,680 BC), but used the most extraordinary assumptions to reach this result.

Lockyer had spent many years studying the relationship between the heavens and various Egyptian temples. When he turned his attention to Stonehenge, instead of trying to make educated guesses about moved stones, he simply plotted a line down the centre of the avenue, making small adjustments for its variation. When he plotted the line, he found it passed close to Sidbury Hill, a hill with an earthwork about eight miles to the north-east. For no

very good reason, he decided to shift his presumed axis of Stonehenge so the two would link up. Then he firmly decided that the first gleam of the rising sun must be the indicator that the structure was built to record, and made his calculations from there.

Lockyer went on to plot other relationships between nearby features from all sorts of periods – since there are so many barrows, earthworks, ridgeways and ruins in the vicinity, it's not hard to produce geometric shapes if you've got a ruler and enough patience. His triangulation of Stonehenge, Old Sarum and Groveley Castle, though, did turn out to predict the path of two of the most powerful ley lines running beneath the UK, or so believers will tell you.

FRED HOYLE

Astronomers were swayed by the accounts of Gerald Hawkins, who argued that Stonehenge was a Neolithic computer, but archaeologists were persuaded less easily. They hit back with details of the markers his theory relied on, some rough pits and chance features of the landscape, not made by man at all. They pointed out that the Aubrey Holes seemed to have been filled in after being dug, so if they were dug to hold marker posts, their use for this function didn't last very long.

One of the most damning counter-charges to this 'computer theory' was the fact that what Hawkins counted as a significant alignment, could be up to two degrees out of true. However, when Fred Hoyle, the celebrated astronomer based at Cambridge University, was invited to examine the problem, not only did he declare that the alignments were off, but they were also deliberately so, and produced observations that were more, not less, precise. He also came up with his own theory of how the Aubrey Holes might have been used to predict eclipses and he declared that the early astronomers who built the original earthworks at Stonehenge must have had great mental faculties.

OLD PICTURE, NEW CAPTION

The design for 'Jellyhenge' never got past the planning stage.

TOP RATED STONE CIRCLES IN ENGLAND...

...according to megalithic.co.uk whose researchers rank each site for overall condition, ambiance and ease of access. Scoring is out of 15, and only those sites which have scored 11 points or more are listed.

Castlerigg, Cumbria, 14
Arbor Low, Derbyshire, 13
Barbrook 1, Derbyshire, 13
Boscawen-Un, Cornwall, 13
Brisworthy, Devon, 13
Mitchells Fold, Shropshire, 13
Nine Stones (Bodmin), Devon, 13
Rollright Stones, Oxfordshire, 13
Bullstones, Cheshire, 12
Doll Tor, Derbyshire, 12
Duloe, Cornwall, 12
Goatstones, Northumberland, 12
Harland Moor, Yorkshire, 12
Lower Piles, Devon, 12
Merry Maidens, Cornwall, 12
Nine Stones (Belstone), Devon, 12
Nine Stones Close, Derbyshire, 12
Scorhill, Devon, 12
Stoke Flat, Derbyshire, 12
Stonor Park, Oxfordshire, 12
Swinside, Cumbria, 12
The Hurlers, Cornwall, 12
Yellowmead, Devon, 12

Yockenthwaite, Yorkshire, 12
Boskednan, Cornwall, 11
Down Tor, Devon, 11
Drizzlecombe SSE, Devon, 11
Duddo Five Stones, Northumberland, 11
Fernacre, Cornwall, 11
Fernworthy Circle, Devon, 11
Grey Wethers, Devon, 11
Hethpool, Northumberland, 11
Men-An-Tol, Cornwall, 11
Shovel Down Fourfold Circle, Devon, 11
Stannon Circle, Cornwall, 11
Stanton Drew, Somerset, 11
Summerhouse Hill, Lancashire, 11
Trippet Stones, Cornwall, 11
Valley of Stones, Dorset, 11
Crow Hill Cairn Circle, Yorkshire, 11
Mardon Down S, Devon, 11
Wigford Down, Devon, 11

The Danes

Stonehenge puzzled antiquarians from the seventeenth century, because it was more organised and designed than many other rings of standing stones, and there was nothing quite like it to be found in Europe. Major surveys were done of the British Isles, without any similar constructions being uncovered. So they began to cast around for things that might be precursors of the monument – structures and signs of building skill that might hint that the builders went on to create something as noble as Stonehenge.

In Holland, the antiquarians spotted *hunebedden* ('giants graves'), enormous barrows that demonstrated signs of masonic proficiency. However, they were sure (correctly, for once) that the Dutch had never settled in England. In Denmark, there were *dysser*, similarly monumental barrows. Dr Walter Charleton, one of the King's personal physicians, began corresponding with a Danish scholar, Olaus Worm, who had been conducting a study of *dyssers*. Charleton became convinced that these were the prototype constructions Stonehenge scholars had been looking for, and promptly wrote a thesis suggesting that the Danes had done the deed in the ninth century.

Stonehenge wasn't a temple, according to Charleton, but a place where the Danish kings were crowned. This suited the mood perfectly in 1663, when Charles II had only been restored to the throne for three years. The notion that the country's most spellbinding ancient monument had been built to honour its kings was undoubtedly tempting. But common sense soon began to ask difficult questions (such as why, if it was constructed comparatively recently, were there no records either in English or Danish histories, of Stonehenge's erection?) and after enjoying a brief vogue the idea soon fell out of the popular consciousness.

QUOTE UNQUOTE

The highways and the main streets of old towns in summer are as crowded as Piccadilly and far noisier. Moreover, everything supposedly beautiful or interesting is exploited for admission charges. Stonehenge has a barbed-wire fence round it and a turnstile. At the Devil's Bridge notices read: 'One shilling to see the landscape immortalised by Wordsworth'.
Richard Aldington, author, writing in
Life for Life's Sake: A Book of Reminiscences

Appas went to his chamber, and this mischief meditated; he was a heathen man, out of Saxland come. Monk's clothes he took on, he shaved his crown upon; he took to him two companions, and forth he gan proceed, and went anon right into Winchester, as if it were a holy man – the heathen devil! He went to the burgh-gate, where the king lay in chamber, and greeted the door-keeper with God's greeting; and bade him in haste go into the king, and say to him in sooth, that Uther his brother had sent him thither a good leech; the best leech that dwelt in any land, that ever any sick man out of sickness can bring. Thus he lied, the odious man, to the monarch, for Uther was gone forth with his army, nor ever him saw Uther, nor thither him sent! And the king weened that it were sooth, and believed him enow. Who would ween that he were traitor! – for on his bare body he wore a cuirass, thereupon he had a loathly haircloth, and then a cowl of a black cloth; he had blackened his body, as if smutted with coal! He kneeled to the king, his speech was full mild: 'Hail be thou, Aurelie, noblest of all kings! Hither me sent Uther, that is thine own brother; and I all for God's love am here to thee come. For I will heal, and all whole thee make, for Christ's love, God's son; I reck not any treasure, nor meed of land, nor of silver nor of gold, but to each sick person I do it for love of my Lord.' The king heard this, it was to him most agreeable; – but where is ever any man in this middle-earth, that

would this ween, that he were traitor! He took his glass vessel anon, and the king urined therein; a while after that, the glass vessel in hand he took, and viewed it forth-right before the king's knights; and thus said anon Appas, the heathen man: 'If ye will me believe, ere to-morrow eve this king shall be all whole, healed at his will.' Then were blithe all that were in chamber. Appas went in a chamber, and the mischief meditated, and put thereto poison, that hight scamony, and came out forth-right among the chamber-knights, and to the knights he gan to distribute much canel, and gingiver and liquorice he gave them lovingly. They all took the gift, and he deceived them all. This traitor fell on his knees before the monarch, and thus said to him: 'Lord, now thou shalt receive this, of this drink a part, and that shall be thy cure.' And the king up drank, and there the poison he drank. Anon as he had drank, the leech laid him down. Thus said Appas to the chamberknights: 'Wrap now the king well, that he lie in sweating; for I say to you through all things, all whole shall your king be. And I will go to my inn, and speak with my men, and at the midnight I will come again forth-right, with other leechcraft, that shall be to him healing.' Forth went – while the king lay in slumber – the traitor Appas to his inn, and spake with his men; and with stilly counsel stole from the town.

Wace Layamon,
Arthurian Chronicles, **1912**

MOOD MUSIC

When you want to suggest moody depth to your music, and display your folk credentials, sticking a shot of some lichen-patched standing stones on the cover of your album certainly does the trick. From the famous to the unheard of, they've all tried it...

Van Morrison, *The Philosopher's Stone*
Rather splendid stormy photo of the Stones of Stenness

Clannad, *Magical Ring*
Photo of the Piper's Stone in Ireland

Les Barker, *The Stones of Callanish*
Photo of Callanish I

Ultravox, *Lament*
Black and white photo of Callanish I

Paul McCartney, *Standing Stone*
Photo of unidentified monolith, shot by his late wife Linda

ANCIENT ORDER OF DRUIDS

The Ancient Order of Druids didn't manage to hold a ceremony at Stonehenge until 1905, when around 650 of them turned up for a mass initiation. For a lot of middle class men at the time, being a Druid was probably on a par with joining the Masons – a night away from the wife, a bit of mystical tomfoolery, a chance to dress up and perhaps, most importantly, to take advantage of the chance to network with comfortable businessmen of his own class. Going to Stonehenge to be initiated must have seemed like the ultimate jolly.

They turned up with loads of food and drink and put up a refreshment marquee, and used a secret password to keep curious bystanders away, very *Boys' Own* adventure. In total, 258 novices were present, including Sir Edmund Antrobus who had accepted their invitation to come and be initiated. After feasting in the refreshment tent, the initiates were taken off and blindfolded, while everyone else slipped into white hooded robes and bushy beards (if they didn't already have their own growth, one can only presume. Certainly people were advertising 'Druidical' beards at the time).

To a specially composed anthem the initiates snaked their way into the circle, where GA Lardner, Most Noble Grand Arch Brother of the Order, was waving his battleaxe over a sacred fire. After Lardner had uttered the sacred oath, off came the blindfolds and everyone had a singsong of the anthem and, one suspects, a hearty hug.

STUKELEY'S WORMS

After studying the ancient monuments and earthworks of Great Britain, and, in particular, those around Stonehenge, Dr William Stukeley – antiquarian, cabalist and Druid-lover extraordinaire – developed a theory that when viewed as a whole, the various large features on the landscape made up giant serpents or worms. This, to him, explained the propensity for large circles to be found with avenues leading to and from them. He named such circles Dracontia: Dragon Temples.

Because so many ancient British sites are associated with dragons and dragon slayers in folklore, Stukeley was able to 'join the dots' between many locations where fiery beasts and giant 'wurms' had been said to reside, kept treasure or been slain. At the time, vestiges of rituals associated with dragon slaying were alive and well in the form of Mumming plays and thinly disguised pagan seasonal festivities, so it's no wonder Stukeley began seeing dragons on the land.

Despite having no way of observing from the air, he quickly perceived a number of these huge dragon figures in various parts of the country, including Callanish in the Outer Hebrides. His book on Avebury is illustrated with a drawing of the stone circle and earthworks there as the, admittedly, rather swollen belly of a giant serpent, whose head rests below and to the east on The Sanctuary at Overton Hill, a wooden henge that once featured six concentric circles of uprights, but is now, sadly, destroyed.

CASTING THE RUNES

Which noted architect described Stonehenge as 'The Most Notable Antiquity of Great Britain'?
a) Christopher Wren
b) Frank Lloyd Wright
c) Inigo Jones
d) Le Corbusier
Answer on page 153.

QUOTE UNQUOTE

One of the great stones that lies downe, on the west side, hath a cavity something resembling the print of a man's food: concerning which the Shepherds and Countrey people have a Tradition (which many of them doe steadfastly believe) that when Marlin conveyed these Stones from Ireland by Art Magick, the Devill hitt him in the heele with that stone, and so left the print there.
John Aubrey, antiquary and writer, writing in
Monumenta Britannica, 1670s

FREE FESTIVAL FIENDS

The Stonehenge Free Festival attracted a number of festival habitués, as well as some chart bands with indie leanings. Here are some of the performers that mainstream music fans may have heard of:

Crass (festival founders)
Hawkwind • Misty in Roots
The Selector • Sugar Minott
Theatre of Hate • Thompson Twins

STONEHENGE ON TV

Quatermass and the Pit
Still genuinely spooky, this 1979 continuation of the *Quatermass* series is set in a dystopian future where science is being forgotten and machinery is breaking down, and has the young people of Earth mysteriously drawn to stone circles around the world, where they believe they'll be taken up by benign aliens. Only Professor Quatermass understands the aliens are anything from nice.

Xena: Warrior Princess
Xena, along with her friend Gabrielle, rescues a British slave who enlists their help to overthrow Julius Caesar. They meet Boudicca and fall foul of an evil cult. In blowing up the cult's temple, they manage to leave just a few stones standing, to form Stonehenge.

Eddie Izzard: Dress to Kill
Recording of a San Francisco performance that includes the UK's favourite transvestite comedian's erudite routine on paganism and early Christianity, the building of Stonehenge and medieval Western European empires.

Tess of the D'Urbervilles
Loving 1998 TV adaptation of the Thomas Hardy novel by Ted Whitehead, directed by Ian Sharp. Appears to feature the actual stones, rather than models!

Relic Hunter
Lara Croft-esque series, in episode 66 of which the 'bootilicious' treasure hunters visit England and are tricked into searching for the 'Keys to Stonehenge' on behalf of an evil secret society.

Ravena, the Goddess of Stonehenge
OK, so her show didn't actually feature Stonehenge, but it's too good a name to pass up. Ravena was a buxom blonde horror show host in the grand American tradition of Elvira and Vampira who, with her sidekick Anok, presented camp horror films to a post-watershed audience on Friday nights in the late 1990s.

COUNTRIES WITH THE MOST
WORLD HERITAGE SITES

1 Italy (40)
2 Spain (38)
3= Germany and China (31)
5 France (30)
6= India and UK (26)
8 Mexico (25)
9 Russia (23)
10 USA (20)

'IS THAT ALL?'

But is it not wonderful that I am here in this remote and interesting and storied spot? – the last retreat of the little people called fairies, the lurking-place of giants and enchanters.... At Stonehenge we found a few rude stones for a temple. I could not gather into a small enough focus the wide glances of Julian's great brown, searching eyes to make him see even what there was; and when finally he comprehended that the circle of stones once marked out a temple, and that the Druids really once stood there, he curled his lip, scornfully exclaiming, 'Is that all?' and bounded off to pluck flowers. I think that, having heard of Stonehenge and a Druid temple which was built of stones so large that it was considered almost miraculous that they were moved to their places, he expected to see a temple touching the sky, perhaps.... Mr Hawthorne came back the next Friday, much to our joy, and on Saturday afternoon we walked to the Nunnery with him, which was founded by St Bridget. A few ruins remain, overgrown with old ivy vines of such enormous size that I think they probably hold the walls together.... Julian and Una were enchanted with the clear stream, and Julian was wild for turtles; but there are no reptiles in the Isle of Man.... I kept thinking, 'And this is the rugged, bare, rocky isle which I dreaded to come to, – this soft, rich, verdant paradise!' It really seems as if the giants had thrown aloft the bold, precipitous rocks and headlands round the edge of the island, to guard the sylvan solitudes for the fairies, whose stronghold was the Isle of Man. I should not have been surprised at any time to have seen those small people peeping out of the wild foxgloves, which are their favorite hiding-places. So poetical is the air of these regions that mermaids, fairies, and giants seem quite natural to it.

Rose Hawthorne Lathrop,
Memories of Hawthorne, 1897

AND COUNTRIES WITH ONLY ONE
WORLD HERITAGE SITE

Andorra • Azerbaijan • Bahrain • Belize
Benin • Bosnia and Herzegovina • Botswana
Cambodia • Cameroon • Central African Republic
Democratic People's Republic of Korea
Dominica • Dominican Republic • Gambia
Guinea • Haiti • Iceland • Luxembourg
Macedonia • Malawi • Mozambique
Nicaragua • Paraguay • Republic of Moldova
Slovenia • Saint Kitts and Nevis
Solomon Islands • St Lucia • Sudan
Togo • Uruguay • Zambia

KEEPERS OF THE STONES

Since 1984, Stonehenge has been in the keeping of English Heritage, a government body whose purpose is, according to its stated aims, to manage 'the historic environment of England', as well as to ensure the public have access to places of historic significance and educational materials to understand them.

Formerly the Historic Buildings and Monuments Commission for England, English Heritage was set up as a not-for-profit organisation in 1983, following the passing of the National Heritage Act in 1983. English Heritage is funded by the Department for Culture, Media and Sports (DCMS), as well as deriving income from some of its more popular venues via entry fees. English Heritage is primarily responsible for the built environment rather than the landscape itself (which is the remit of its complementary organisation, English Nature), starting with the early menhirs and stone circles, and covering every kind of structure. Similar to the National Trust, English Heritage is responsible for the upkeep of many beautiful and significant buildings, but, unlike the former, it is not a charity.

English Heritage registers structures of historical importance, gives advice on how to deal with them, and undertakes conservation programmes where necessary. In some instances, such as Stonehenge, English Heritage owns the site, but in others, it undertakes the stewardship of privately owned structures, or simply advises owners on what is the best practice. English Heritage regularly advises the Office of the Deputy Prime Minister, and the Departments for the Environment, Food and Rural Affairs and for Trade and Industry on areas such as the listing of buildings and the scheduling of ancient monuments.

Some believe that ley lines are energy paths which run in straight lines across the landscape. The power of these lines, it is believed, drew ancient peoples to create roads along them, and to construct significant structures on them. They are usually over a mile long, but can run on for several miles. Where they cross, energy vortices occur. This is believed to be the case at Stonehenge.

In modern terms, the idea for ley lines comes from Alfred Watkins, a Herefordshire businessman who, after studying a map on 30 June 1921, noticed that he could connect many ancient points of interest with straight lines. He later discovered that old tracks often existed along these lines, and that they met and branched off, running all over the country. He just presumed they were prehistoric trading routes.

The association with pathways of power appears to come from occult writer Dion Fortune, who mentions them in her 1936 novel *The Goat-Footed God*, but it wasn't until a decade or so later that the idea they were routes for earth energy became prevalent.

Proponents of ley lines believe several grids of electromagnetic energy run around the Earth (there are also, for instance, hartmann lines, curry lines and benker lines), which can be detected by dowsing. The two main British lines, the St Michael and St Mary leys, pass through many sacred sites, including Glastonbury.

The major ley line through Stonehenge (although there are believed to be several radiating out from it) is known as the Stonehenge Ley, and was first discovered by the astronomer Sir Norman Lockyer (and extended by KH Koop) when he was triangulating ancient monuments. The ley line enters the Sarsen circle at stone 19 and exits at 27, then continues along the first section of the avenue.

STONEHENGE WAS BUILT BY...

Teenagers

Many studies have devoted close attention to the problem of how and why Neolithic man transported the vast stones incorporated into the monument across miles of countryside. Fewer have paid much attention as to the identity of those who actually did the hauling. But, as American historian Mary Laine points out, life expectancy among the builders of the stone circle was dramatically shorter than it is today: a 30-year-old, in 3,000 BC, would have been considered venerable. So, who built Stonehenge? 'Forty per cent of the people who lived then probably died before the age of 20,' Laine says. 'Therefore, it is most likely that Stonehenge was built by teenagers.'

BUSH BARROW ARTEFACTS

William Cunnington uncovered some of the most magnificent artefacts left behind by the Ancient Britons when he opened a very large bowl barrow known as Bush Barrow on Normanton Down, about a mile south of Stonehenge. As a whole, the Normanton Down barrows are the richest barrows ever excavated. In the Bush Barrow alone, Cunnington and his team discovered:

- Two decorated lozenge-shaped plates made entirely of gold
- A gold belt hook
- Two metal daggers, the handle of one decorated with thousands of tiny gold pins
- A bronze axe
- A bronze lance head
- A stone mace head
- Bone mounts
- Bronze rivets
- Wood and bronze fragments, possibly from a shield

MEDIEVAL STONEHENGE

Most of the legends associated with Stonehenge grew up in the Medieval period, and the first lengthy account of the site is as a backdrop to battles and massacres. The structure was supposed to be a tomb for legendary figures such as Uther Pendragon, and/or a monument erected by Uther to commemorate the Roman-British knights, possibly led by Vortigern, who were massacred by the Saxons led by Hengist, around 462 AD.

In the pages of the *Domesday Book,* Stonehenge is recorded as being part of a royal estate, and its next mention is in Henry of Huntingdon's *The History of the English People 1000-1154,* from around 1130, where he calls it 'Stanenges'. Six years later,

Geoffrey of Monmouth's *History of the Kings of Britain* embellished Henry's mere description with stories of betrayal, war and magic, and popularised the modern spelling Stonehenge. Many medieval chroniclers, such as Wace (*Roman de Brut,* 1155), Peter Langtoft (*Chronicle,* c. 1307) and Robert Mannyng of Brunne (*Chronicle,* 1338), repeat Geoffrey's tales, subtly altering them to reflect on then-current political and social currents.

While all this writing was taking place, Stonehenge saw few visitors other than the shepherds who were watching the king's sheep, which were grazing on Salisbury Plain. Stonehenge's role as a tourist attraction was still many years away.

John Aubrey, who gave his name to the 56 holes cut just inside the enclosing earthwork of Stonehenge, wrote a study of ancient structures, but it was never published in his lifetime. Even his most famous book, the *Lives of Eminent Men*, a series of haphazard biographical sketches, wasn't published until 126 years after he died.

He was born near Malmesbury in Wiltshire to a wealthy family, and as a boy studied under Robert Latimer, who also taught Thomas Hobbes. Aubrey's university education was interrupted by the Civil War. On his father's death in 1652, he inherited the heavily encumbered family estates which, in a series of court cases, he lost over the ensuing 18 years.

Aubrey mixed with a glittering array of writers, politicians and men of letters. He joined the Royal Society and the Rotary Club and, when he lost his family home in 1670 and was reliant on the hospitality of friends, he was taken on by the painstaking antiquarian Anthony Wood to gather material for his *Athenae Oxonienses: an Exact History of all the Writers and Bishops who have had their Education in the University of Oxford from 1500 to 1690*. Aubrey inundated him with sketches and notes. He lived in a variety of noblemen's houses, and was able to scour their libraries for interesting tidbits. Never a great organiser of information, his notes are full of instructions to 'look it up later', but he did set great store by personal observation and accurate transcription of even the most trifling of conversations. Rather than taking someone's word for it, he liked to see things for himself.

Aubrey never published most of his best work. He began a *History of Northern Wiltshire*, but handed his research over to Thomas Tanner in 1695, when he felt he was too old to complete it. He wrote on local antiquities during his travels; his notes on Surrey were published as part of R Rawlinson's *Natural History and Antiquities of Surrey*, 1719, and those on Wiltshire were published as part of *Wiltshire: the Topographical Collections* by JE Jackson, 1862.

But to students of Stonehenge, it is his unpublished *Monumenta Britannica* that is important, containing notes on Avebury, Stonehenge, Waylands Smithy and other prehistoric structures. He was the first to recognise that the Avebury stones were all part of the same temple, and described Stonehenge as a temple built by 'the Priests of the most eminent Order, viz, Druids'. He also recorded the presence of slight indentations in the ground around the inner ring of the earthwork surrounding Stonehenge. It would be nearly 300 years before anyone realised the importance of this observation, when archaeologists led by William Hawley and Robert Newell realised they were a circle of holes cut into the chalk there, originally to hold large wooden posts, but later filled in and used for burials.

'A Week at Land's End', JT Blight, 1861

BEST OF BRITISH

Bryn Cader Faner, Llanfair, Gwynedd

Burial sites in Wales seem to share an awareness of location not found in other countries. Perhaps the most beautifully situated is Bryn Cader Faner, a cairn on a rocky ridge, positioned so that visitors who are approaching from the south would suddenly come upon it. It's rather a long walk from the nearest road (about two miles, although it is a pretty ramble), and visitors are advised to take a detailed map, stout boots and a compass. The ancient approach route is now rather boggy, and there's nary a signpost. It's worth reading the experiences of other visitors online to help orientate yourself before setting off to find it.

The cairn lies at the centre of a small stone circle, about 8.5 metres wide. It rises less than a metre, and around it, like the points of a giant crown, are 15 slabs which lean outwards from its low mound. The 15 stones, each about two metres long, give the site a sense of ethereality, whereas most monuments from this period impress by their vast size and immovable weightiness.

Originally there may have been up to 30 stones, but, unfortunately, Bryn Cader Faner has been disturbed several times. In addition to the workings of time, at some point during the nineteenth century, a shaft was dug into the cairn itself and it appears a cist or something similar was removed, leaving the burial chamber open to the elements. Then, during World War II, the army came along and removed some of the stones on the east side for reasons unknown.

Druids all wear white dresses
While modern Druids are fond of long robes, not all of them wear white. Different orders like different colours. And you can even wear trousers underneath.

Ancient Druids cut sacred mistletoe with gold sickles
No one has ever dug up a golden sickle. Gold is a soft metal, so it wouldn't have made an ideal blade. It's likely that if the Romans saw Druids using something gilt-coloured and shiny, it was copper or bronze.

Druids must have long beards
This goes back to the great patriarch idea and yes, a lot of Druids from the last 300 years have sported big, bushy Father Christmas-style facial fur (particularly in the Victorian period, when this was the norm for the more mature man), but it's not mandatory.

Druids are essentially medicine men
Although they did have a function as healers, the *Asterix* stories seem to have planted this idea firmly in most people's minds. In fact, the original Druids were a ruling elite of priests as involved with politics and the judicial system as with teaching and medicine (although they did play a big part in these areas also).

The Ancient Druids worshipped at Stonehenge
Despite what the modern ones would like us to believe, there is little evidence that they did. Roman accounts agree that Druids worshipped in groves, specifically oak groves, holding, according to Pliny 'nothing more sacred than mistletoe and the tree on which it is growing'.

Druids always cut mistletoe from oak trees
Druids might like to have cut it from here in an ideal world, but, in reality, mistletoe is rarely found growing on oak trees (the Romans noted this, too, so it's not something that's happened as a result of deforestation). When Druids did find mistletoe on an oak, it was gathered with special ceremony.

QUOTE UNQUOTE

In choosing Stonehenge as the setting for her last hours with Angel, Hardy stressed the sacrificial elements involved, but he looked upon Tess as having been destroyed by 'the letter of a law that killeth'. I do not think he was fully aware of the significance of his symbolism, of that which he had rightly apprehended with his intuition.
Evelyn Hardy, writing in *Thomas Hardy: A Critical Biography*

The largest stone circle in the world, according to the *Guinness Book of Records*, is in:

a) France

b) England

c) Peru

d) Egypt

e) Tahiti

Answer on page 153.

A PR PROBLEM

They used no images to represent the object of their worship, nor did they meet in temples or buildings of any kind for the performance of their sacred rites. A circle of stones (each stone generally of vast size), enclosing an area of from twenty feet to thirty yards in diameter, constituted their sacred place. The most celebrated of these now remaining is Stonehenge, on Salisbury Plain, England.

These sacred circles were generally situated near some stream, or under the shadow of a grove or widespreading oak. In the centre of the circle stood the Cromlech or altar, which was a large stone, placed in the manner of a table upon other stones set up on end. The Druids had also their high places, which were large stones or piles of stones on the summits of hills. These were called Cairns, and were used in the worship of the deity under the symbol of the sun.

That the Druids offered sacrifices to their deity there can be no doubt. But there is some uncertainty as to what they offered, and of the ceremonies connected with their religious services we know almost nothing. The classical (Roman) writers affirm that they offered on great occasions human sacrifices; as for success in war or for relief from dangerous diseases. Cæsar has given a detailed account of the manner in which this was done. 'They have images of immense size, the limbs of which are framed with twisted twigs and filled with living persons. These being set on fire, those within are encompassed by the flames.' Many attempts have been made by Celtic writers to shake the testimony of the Roman historians to this fact, but without success.

Thomas Bulfinch, *Bulfinch's Mythology: The Age of Fable; The Age of Chivalry; Legends of Charlemagne*, 1913

LET THERE BE... ROCK!

Although Neolithic monuments have proved popular imagery with rock bands and folksters alike, Stonehenge itself hasn't turned up so often. Here's just a few places that the iconic stones have been used on modern album covers.

Hawkwind, *This is Hawkwind, Do Not Panic*
White illustration of the inner circle, on a crushed raspberry ground. Nice

Alan Stivell, Symphonie Celtique, *Tir Na N-og*
Moody sunset photograph of the main circle

Calverly, Avalon, *Celtic Mysteries, Celtic Mysteries II*
Pseudo Celtic decorative scrolling with different circular portraits in the centre of each. Very 1970s

Mike Simmons, *Compositions of Stone*
Close-up photo of Stonehenge

The Rough Guide to English Roots Music
Modern, sunny photo of the stones compiled with other images

THE STONES OF BLOOD

In his travels through time and space, the Doctor (*Doctor Who*) has only once encountered Stonehenge – or rather a Stonehenge-style circle called the 'Nine Travellers', actually shot at the Rollright Stones in Oxfordshire. Writer David Fisher combines several Stonehenge legends in this four-part story, which sees the fourth Doctor (Tom Baker) and the first Romana (Mary Tamm) looking for one of the six segments to the Key to Time. The time travellers have already got two bits, and their sensors guide them to the stone circle, where they're met by dotty Professor Amelia Rumford and her assistant, the significantly named Vivien Fay.

The duo explain to the Doctor that no matter how many times they survey the stones, the number seems to change (my guess would be nine), and many people have also seen the stones in different locations. Enter, stage left, a party of mysterious modern Druids, led by a man called de Vries, who worship the Cailleach, a Celtic goddess of war. It turns out that the stones are an ancient race of blood-loving aliens, the Ogri, who demand human sacrifice, and the 'goddess' is an interstellar criminal who's been using their power for her own evil ends. A couple of campers and de Vries come to a bloody end, before the Doctor solves the mystery of the Stones of Blood...

To behold this 'wonder of Britain' it should be viewed with an artist's eye, and contemplated by an intellect stored with antiquarian and historical knowledge.
Edgar Allen Poe, author, writing in 'Some Account of Stonehenge, The Giant's Dance, A Druidical Ruin in England', *Burton's Gentleman's Magazine*, June 1840

STONEHENGE WAS BUILT BY...

The Phoenicians

Slightly more real than the Atlantean architects dreamed up by some historians of Stonehenge, were the Phoenicians. Once the arguments over the rival claims of the Romans and Danes to have been the builders of Stonehenge were exhausted, indefatigable seventeenth-century historians began casting around for other possible builders and seemed to favour those about whom the least was known. Of course, one might say, the less was known the less untidy and contradictory facts might be unearthed.

The Phoenicians, a Semitic people from an area that now covers parts of Syria and Lebanon, called their country Canaan and themselves the Canaani or Kennaini. But because they were famous traders and seafarers who transported exotic Tyrian purple dye they became known to the Greeks as the Phoniki, or purple people, and the name stuck. During the first millennium BC, they spread across the Mediterranean so, some scholars thought, it wasn't such a leap to have them visit Britain and found a colony here. In fact some modern historians believe they did reach Cornwall and traded there for tin, which was in demand to make bronze, but there is little evidence to support this claim.

Aylett Sammes, in his *Britannia Antiqua Illustrata* (1676), commenting on Geoffrey of Monmouth's account of the building of Stonehenge suddenly states 'Why may not these Giants, so often mentioned, upon this, and other occasions, be the Phoenicians [...] and the art of erecting these stones [...] bought from the farthermost parts of Africa, the known habitation of the Phoenicians.' Sammes had absolutely no proof – the Phoenicians weren't giants, he had no evidence they'd visited Britain (and certainly not, as he later went on to claim, led by Hercules!) and they didn't appear to build large round monuments. Nonetheless, their very mysteriousness, and known wanderlust, led many prominent people to give the theory brain-room, at least for a few years.

IOLO MORGANWG,
AKA EDWARD WILLIAMS (1747-1826)

Iolo Morganwg – forger, convict, revolutionary – is without doubt the father of modern Druidism. It was he who established the first revival meeting and poetry contest on 21 June 1792, not amid the stones of Stonehenge, but in Primrose Hill. Morganwg invented much of the ritual that is still followed by Druids today. Morganwg's Druids didn't go around slaughtering anything, much less burning people in wicker cages à la *Wicker Man*. He established Druidism as a broad church, embracing a range of teachings and emphasising nature's holiness.

Taking 'Ned of Glamorgan' as his bardic name, Morganwg set out to prove the Druidic tradition had been handed down, secretly, through the generations from Celtic Britain and preserved by the Welsh – particularly the Southern Welsh, since he had been born in Llancarfan, Glamorgan. He also promoted the idea Welsh explorer Madoc had been the first white man to discover America, which received enough support for an expedition to be dispatched to the Midwest to look for signs of Welshness.

Morganwg gathered together elements of Celtic tradition which had survived the Roman and Tudor purges, and then manufactured other sources, forging ancient texts to support his claims. His books include *Cyfrinach Beirdd Ynys Prydain* (*The Mysteries or Secrets of the Bards of the Isle of Britain*), which it is believed he forged while he was in a debtors' prison for a year in the 1780s. With the help of this and other documents, he persuaded Welsh literary circles in London that he was heir to the great Druidic tradition of their homeland, and got several of his ancient manuscripts published. On his death he was working on *The History of the British Bards*, the papers from which are now held by the National Library of Wales.

Addicted to laudanum most of his adult life, Morganwg's vision of a Celtic religion is very much in keeping with the times when Romanticism was at its height. The popularity of his Gorsedd also reflects a fondness for secret societies and gentlemen's clubs that gave us the Masons and the Rosicrucians, for example.

His ideas continued to attract ardent followers throughout the nineteenth century and into the middle of the twentieth, thanks to a collection, *The Barddas of Iolo Morganwg*, put together by J Williams Ab Ithel. But it wasn't until Professor Griffith John Williams, professor of Welsh at University College, Cardiff, made a detailed examination of his papers that he was caught out. Even to this day, it is hard to identify which parts are based on genuine medieval documents and which refer to forgeries.

142 *Catalogue number of George Crumb's avant-garde* Makrokosmos I and II *which contains* Ghost-Nocturne: for the Druids of Stonehenge

AN ARTIST'S VIEW

An early megalithic illustration,
unknown artist, 1769

SPOOKY STONEHENGE

Stonehenge surges

Stonehenge is situated (according to believers) on the vortex of several ley lines – ancient lines of earth energy that run all over the globe. One of these unseen power lines runs for 22 miles, from the River Avon to the monument, bisecting the Heel Stone. Whether it's energy from the ley line, another mystical force, or just desire on the part of the observers, a lot of people record feeling surges of energy when standing among or near the stones. These surges make their hair stand on end and their whole body feel enervated. Some put it down to the type of granite much of Wiltshire and the equally paranormally active Cornwall sit on, and others think it's to do with solar energy.

One oft-repeated story concerns a man flying a kite near the car park at Stonehenge. For some reason he decided to stand on his vehicle, so he was no longer earthed, at which point his kite flew over the monument. A mysterious force then seemed to travel down the kite and zap his hands, and the man was rendered unconscious, but news reports are extremely vague on the details. Unspecified wounds took six months to heal. All in all, it sounds rather like a lightning strike.

THE BARDIC ALPHABET

As well as giving Druidism a wide range of source materials, many of which he invented himself, Iolo Morganwg also created the Bardic alphabet, which is a mixture of Runic symbols and the ancient Celtic Ogham symbol system.

Iolo Morganwg's son, Taliesin, won the Abergavenny Essay prize for an essay at the 1838 Eisteddfod, which defended the Bardic alphabet. This was published in 1840 and was widely read. But even then, some people were beginning to question the veracity of his father's sources. But it appears Taliesin was genuine in his belief that the original tale he spread was from an actual source, although the content is clearly meant to be allegorical.

In the tale, Einigan Gawr sees three rays of light on which all knowledge is inscribed, which became known as the Bardic symbol, the Awen (or 'inspiration' in Welsh). Einigan takes three rods of mountain ash or rowan and writes on them all the knowledge the rods of light contain, but people don't believe him, so he breaks the ash rods and dies. A year and a day after his death, Menw ab Teirgwaedd (a figure from the tale of *Culhwych and Olwen* in *The Mabinogion*) sees three staffs growing out of the mouth of Einigan's dead body, which have all the knowledge of the Druids written on them except for the name of God, which is the great Druidic secret.

WHILE YOU'RE IN THE AREA WHY NOT VISIT...

The Merchant's House

Often the best way to bring history alive, especially for children, is to recreate everyday life at a certain date, down to the tiniest of details. While the clashing of armies on battlefields may be hard for a young mind to picture, surrounded by evidence of ordinary life to which they can relate, their imagination will be fired up.

The Merchant's House in Marlborough is a recreation of the home of a silk merchant, Thomas Bayly, restored to how it would have looked in 1675. The house had been built in 1653 following a great fire, which had destroyed large parts of Marlborough. Exceedingly stylish at the time, it featured a massive oak staircase and beautiful wall paintings which are still being restored. From the shop to the servant's cramped quarters, the house's own brew house, and the rooms where the family would have lived and slept, it brings the past vividly to life. Visitors can listen to music of the period that the family would have enjoyed, see demonstrations of how clothes were made and discover that the popular image of Puritan life is much duller and darker than the reality.

During the third millennium before Christ, towards the end of that millennium, great stone monuments were being erected in this country on a scale implying considerable wealth, a high degree of political organisation, and a very definite system of religious beliefs.

RG Collingwood and JNL Myers, English philosophers and historians, writing in *Roman Britain and the English Settlements*

SHAPING THE STONES

There were three stages of shaping and finishing required before the builders of Stonehenge were satisfied with the results and ready to erect each stone – each stage requiring a huge amount of time and effort on their part.

1. Rough dressing

This may well have been done on the Marlborough Downs, before the stones were moved (presumably to get rid of any excess weight). Sarsens are naturally slab-like and tend to have at least one pair of sides that are roughly parallel. The most primitive way of splitting great slabs of such hard rock was still being used by locals in the eighteenth century. It involved lighting small fires in a line where you wished to split the rock, and when it was heated throwing cold water over it. The contraction of the particles, combined with some vigorous hammering with large stones, often succeeded in cracking it.

2. Fine shaping

Large hammers with Sarsen heads were used to chip away at the resultant monolith, until the desired shape was achieved. Being so hard, hammering on it tends to produce no more than a little dust and some fine chips so ancient man developed a technique of hammering out a series of long grooves, then working at right angles to the surface to shear off the resultant ridges. The tenons were cut using small quartzite stones as hammers, and the mortises ground out by applying damp sand and using this to grind away the Sarsen. You can only imagine the patience of the builders faced with such jobs.

3. Surfacing

Not content with shaping the stones so carefully, the builders of Stonehenge then began surfacing some of the faces of the stone with a tiny, even texture which was made by using small quartzite hammers. Most of this careful texturalisation has been worn away by the elements, but it can still be spotted in some areas which have been sufficiently protected.

BEST CRACKPOT THEORIES

Giant clock dial – Ludovic McLellan Mann. Exponent of telluric energy theory (a Germanic version of Feng Shui).

Crop circle marker – some Wiccans believe that not only is Stonehenge built at a ley line energy vortex, but it was also patterned after a 'faerie ring' or crop circle.

Fertility symbol in the shape of a vagina – Anthony Perks, a Canadian gynaecologist and headline-grabber. His suggestion is that it's a menstrual calendar.

Serpent worshipper's temple – William Stukeley, a Druid revisionist.

Building in the Garden of Eden – Henry Browne and others believed Stonehenge was antediluvian, but one American even claimed Salisbury Plain was the Garden of Eden.

Thirteen-month calendar – Moses Cotsworth, Director of the International Fixed Calendar League.

UFO landing pad – a claim made for stone circles in general.

Number map – the dimensions of Stonehenge provide many 'significant' numbers which turn up in all aspects of life, according to many numerologists.

Portal to other dimensions, cosmic and afterlife communications system – Steve Travis, experimental Californian builder.

SPOOKY STONEHENGE

Cropping up

Stonehenge and its surrounding monuments seem to attract strange phenomena. Not only are UFOs often seen in the area, but Wiltshire is also considered crop circle central. In 2000, 70 out of 175 crop circles reported in England were found in Wiltshire, many centred around the Avebury and Stonehenge area. The county even has its own monthly crop circle magazine, *The Spiral*, put out by the Wiltshire Crop Circle Study Group. The biggest crop circle ever recorded, which was 787 feet across and covered about five hectares of field, was in the area.

Some people suggest that Wiltshire attracts this activity because of its long history of human habitation, others say it is freak whirlwinds that shape the corn, while others prefer the theory that even the most complex designs are down to the work of hoaxers, who are keen to draw tourists or to make some sort of statement. Perhaps the bottom line is that Wiltshire, with all its ancient history and mystical significance, simply draws the kind of modern inhabitants who want to see aliens, ghosts and strange phenomena more than the rest of us.

Charles Dickens, in an uncharacteristically sloppy journalistic moment, repeated the story that the stones of Stonehenge were uncountable. But he also made a more fabulous claim. According to Dickens, if you stood in the centre, counted the stones 27 times and then said 'I dare', what would happen?

a) You'd see amazing visions then drop dead
b) The Devil would appear and grant you a wish
c) You'd wake Merlin from his eon-long sleep
d) A gateway to the underworld would open between the stones

Answer on page 153.

IT'S ALL OVER NOW, BABY BLUE

You know how it is. It sounds like a good idea on paper. Bring together England and Wales for the Millennium. Hark back to the gargantuan efforts of our distant ancestors in creating one of the best-loved structures in the country. And provide a series of great photo opportunities along the way. And after all, it's not *that* far from Pembroke to Wiltshire, is it?

Thus it was that £100,000 of the Heritage Lottery Fund was spent on a project to carry a three-tonne bluestone from the mountains of Preseli in south Wales 240 miles to Stonehenge using prehistoric technology, all to celebrate the year 2000.

Nothing seemed to go right for the project. Progress was slower than expected, the number of volunteers dwindled, the weather was bad, the replica sled, known as a curragh, on which the stone was being pulled broke, and when it reached the sea, just 17 miles away, it broke loose from its restraints and sank at Dale. By the time the stone was rescued by divers, a tug and a crane, the replica boats were found to be damaged, bad weather was setting in, and the project abandoned.

The next year Pembrokeshire County Council took over the task, but couldn't get insurance, so the bluestone was left on the quayside at Milford Docks for over a year before being driven by road to the National Botanical Gardens at Middleton near Carmarthen.

There the bluestone, dubbed 'Elvis Preseli' by journalists, was blessed in June 2004 by local Druid Chris Warwick (also known as Black Crow) who is reported to have felt special powers at two spots in the stone when he passed his hands over it, which are very good for stress and strains.

Unfortunately he wasn't able to procure any more volunteers to drag it closer to Stonehenge. The garden staff have, apparently, been encouraging people to touch the stone for good luck. Given its history you might want to think twice.

THE WELSH WANT IT BACK

Given that the Greeks have been after the return of their marbles for over two centuries, you wonder what hope a small Welsh pressure group have of getting the Stonehenge bluestones returned to Pembrokeshire. Apart from the fact that they have been out of their native country for millennia, there is also the problem of proving that they actually did come from the Preseli Hills in the first place. However back in 2002 the *Western Mail* was very happy to write a rousing story on the subject.

Carreg Glas, the group who launched the campaign, apparently believe the return of the bluestones could help draw more tourists and, through their magical powers, revive Pembrokeshire's failing economy. They were also unhappy at the idea of sending another bluestone to join their lost rocks at Stonehenge to celebrate the Millennium, stating: 'Long before Stonehenge was conceived of, Pembrokeshire bluestones were revered as being adorned with mystical qualities.' But, as Rhys Sinnett of Preseli Plaid Cymru saliently pointed out to reporters: 'We have loads of bluestones left on the Preselis after all. We don't need to drag these back to promote our county.'

MEGALITHS DU MONDE

The Almendres Cromlech Megalithic Complex, Evora, Portugal

In Britain, a cromlech is a barrow, in France, it's a stone circle. But in Portugal, it's come to mean a whole site of Neolithic erections which stretch across an area that measures 60 x 30 metres. The stones at Almendres, about 12 miles west of Evora (itself a World Heritage Site), represent the largest group of menhirs on the Iberian Peninsula, an area rich in Neolithic monuments. Today, you can view two fields of standing stones, 92 in total, many of which have been carved. Just a kilometre away you can see the Almendres Menhir. This stone stands amid olive groves, a tooled pillar with a softly rounded top, taller and more slender than the stones that make up the circles.

Similar to Stonehenge, there were several phases of activity here during the Neolithic period, there is evidence that the two main sites are each arranged to mark a different solstice. Scientists think that about 100 stones were initially raised, but several have been removed over the years. The first area consists of two concentric stone circles, joined to a second area containing two elliptical formations, built slightly up slope and dated later than the circles. It's the stones of the ellipse where most of the carving is concentrated. Although a few of the stones are squared off, the majority are bulbous, carefully shaped, and taper to a base that's narrower than the top.

One can marvel at the ability to fit huge blocks together as if they were wood; mortise and tenon is expected of a cabinetmaker, not stonemasons working with nothing more than round stone mauls, bashing and chipping. And the notion of freestanding lintels boggles the mind; there was nothing like it in prehistoric Europe.

Gerald Hawkins, astronomer, writing in *Beyond Stonehenge*

THE ARCHITECT'S VIEW

Being naturally inclined in my younger years to study the arts of design, I passed into foreign parts to converse with the great masters thereof in Italy; where I applied myself to search out the ruins of those ancient buildings, which in despite of time itself, and violence of barbarians, are yet remaining. Having satisfied myself in these and returning to my native country, I applied my mind more particularly to the study of architecture. Among the ancient monuments whereof, found here, I deemed none more worthy the searching after than this of Stonehenge: not only in regard of the founders thereof, the time when built, the work itself, but also for the rarity of its invention; being different in form from all I had seen before: likewise of as beautiful proportions, as elegant in order and as stately in aspect as any.

King James in his progress the year one thousand six hundred and twenty, being at Wilton and discoursing of this antiquity, I was sent for by the right honourable William, then Earl of Pembroke, and received there his Majesty's command to produce out of mine own practice in architecture and experience in antiquities abroad, what possibly I could discover concerning this of Stonehenge.

You cannot but remember in what manner the ancient inhabitants of this island lived before reduced to civility by the Romans I have formerly delivered: also how they were first instructed by them in several arts and sciences, whereof the Britons, wholly ignorant before the Romans' arrival here and teaching them. I have given you in like manner a full description of this antiquity whereby doubtless it [Stonehenge] doubtless appears to you, as in truth it is, a work built with much art, order and proportion. That the ancient Britons before the discovery of this island by the Romans could not be the founders thereof, by the former reasons, I suppose is clearly manifested. For where art is not, nothing can be performed by art...'

Inigo Jones,
***Stonehenge Restored*, 1651**

In the nineteenth century the (unpaid) guardian of the stones had a long list of things he was supposed to stop happening. Since his livelihood depended on the generosity of visitors giving him tips, we suspect he may not have been too keen to interfere with their merrymaking.

1. To see no damage is done to the stones and the grass
2. To ascertain the names and addresses of any persons so doing
3. Not to allow visitors to picnic inside the stones
4. Not to allow visitors to light fires inside the ditch
5. To request visitors not to put marks or names on the stones
6. To ensure no picketing or feeding of horses allowed between the stones and the ditch
7. To stop visitors leaving rubbish

STONEHENGE WAS BUILT BY...

The Romans

During the seventeenth century, one of the most prevalent theories about who it was that built Stonehenge centred on the Romans. This was largely due to Inigo Jones who, at the behest of the monarch, had undertaken a major survey of the monument. At this time, the majority of Stonehenge enthusiasts, rather than just observing the stones, began looking at several ancient manuscripts, hoping to find some proof of the origin of the structure. Although they found nothing definitive, Jones and the supporters of the Roman ideal did uncover ancient plans for buildings with a similar schema. They were able, with some mathematical quick-stepping, to declare the design of Stonehenge was in accordance with various classical principles. So Stonehenge became a Roman temple to the sun god Coelus, constructed in a robust and stripped-down style befitting its location, but still an example of Classical architecture, albeit somewhat ravaged by the powers of weather and time.

Supporters of the Roman idea (or more properly ideal) wanted to rescue the temple from any links with the barbarous Druids, noting contemporary Roman writers, witnessing the invasion of Britain, talked of the noble Romans cutting the sacred groves of the Druids down and suppressing their sacrificial tendencies. Thus Stonehenge was a product of enlightened man, not pagans. And it couldn't have been built by the Britons after the Romans had departed because everyone knew the country fell back into a dark age where all but the most primitive arts were lost. But, as Christopher Chippindale puts it in his *Stonehenge Complete*, 'Unfortunately, the best thing about this analysis is its nerve'.

To all these questions beginning 'Why?'
there is one short, simple and perfectly
correct answer: We do not know, and we
shall probably never know.
RJC Atkinson

It is very strange that nobody connects Stonehenge with Atlantis. Both exert an enormous attraction to all sorts of mystics, hippies, romantics etceteras.
Stonehenge theorist EJ de Meester

ANSWERS

The answers. As if you needed them.

P11. d)

P24. c)

P30. c)

P39. a)

P44. a)

P57. Ancient tombs sometimes contain dolmen, which are structures made from large capstones supported by two or more stone uprights, sometimes several, to form a long rectangular stone chamber. Whereas a barrow is simply a name for a burial mound, often known as a tumulus, which is usually made of earth or stones heaped over bodies with or without a burial chamber.

P60. b) Thom was a renowned engineer, and Hawkins an astronomer.

P68. Snake or dragon.

P75. 4,400 feet

P87. d)

P92. a) Menhir is a 'long stone' and is the name given to ancient raised stones which are set up alone, rather than in groups or circles. Megalith, which means 'big stone' in Greek, simply means any large standing stone.

P99. b)

P107. d) Although henge comes from hengen, Old English for hanging, in modern usage a henge has come to mean a round bank and ditch – the meaning is taken from the word Stonehenge itself

P119. b)

P124. d) Leuccipotomy refers specifically to cutting the shapes of horses into a hillside and the other two are made up!

P130. c)

P139. b) at Avebury.

P147. a)

Last year in the twelfth century chronicled by Henry of Huntingdon, who gives a first-hand account of Stonehenge

BIBLIOGRAPHY

The Making of Stonehenge, Rodney Castleden, Routledge

Beyond Stonehenge, Gerald S Hawkins, Harper & Row

Megalithomania, John Michell, Thames & Hudson

Stonehenge Complete, Christopher Chippindale,
Thames & Hudson

Stonehenge in Its Landscape: Twentieth Century Excavations,
English Heritage

Stonehenge, A History in Photographs,
Julian Richards, English Heritage

*Standing Stones: Carnac, Stonehenge and the World of
Megaliths*, Jean-Pierre Mohem, Thames & Hudson

Stonehenge, RJC Atkinson, Hamish Hamilton

Stonehenge: Celebration and Subversion,
Andy Worthington, Alternative Albion

Dictionary of Celtic Myth and Legend, Miranda J Green,
Thames & Hudson

The Celtic Heroic Age, Ed John T Koch and John Carey,
Celtic Studies Publications

The Magic Arts in Celtic Britain, Lewis Spence, Constable

*Breaking the Magic Spell: Radical Theories of Folk and
Fairy tales*, Jack Zipes, Heinneman

Mythical Ireland, Michael Dames, Thames & Hudson

Albion: A Guide to Legendary Britain, Jennifer Westwood,
Granada Publishing

Dictionary of Celtic Mythology, Peter Berresford Ellis,
Constable

The Lost Gods of England, Brian Branston,
Thames & Hudson

Fortean Times General Index Issues 1-66, Ed Steve Moore,
John Brown Publishing

The Druids, Peter Berresford Ellis, Constable

The Mabinogian, Ed Gwyn Jones and Thomas Jones, Everyman

Our Countrymen reckon this for one of our wonders and miracles, and much they marvel from whence such huge stones were brought. I am not curious to argue and dispute, but rather to lament with much grief, that the authors of so notable a monument are buried in oblivion.
William Camden, historian and antiquarian, writing on the enigma of Stonehenge, sixteenth century

ACKNOWLEDGEMENTS

We gratefully acknowledge permission to reprint extracts of copyright material in this book from the following authors, publishers and executors:

Extract from The Concept of Time in Psychology: A Resource Book and Annotated Bibliography *by Jon E Roeckelein, © 2000 Greenwood Publishing Group, Inc., Westport, CT. Reproduced by permission.*

Extract from The Magic Arts in Celtic Britain *by Lewis Spence, published by Rider & Co, reprinted by permission of The Random House Group Ltd.*

Thanks also to Judith Antell at Macmillan for checking copyright on Kilvert's Diary 1870-1879: Selections from the Diary of the Rev. Francis Kilvert *and Julie at Pearson Education for providing similar assistance on* The Letters of William Morris to His Family and Friends.

INDEX

FILL YOUR BOOKSHELF AND YOUR MIND

The Birdwatcher's Companion Twitchers, birders and ornithologists are all catered for in this unique book. ISBN 1-86105-833-0

The Cook's Companion Foie gras or fry-ups, this tasty compilation is an essential ingredient in any kitchen. ISBN 1-86105-772-5

The Countryside Companion From milking stools to crofters tools, this book opens the lid on the rural scene. ISBN 1-86105-918-3

The Fishing Companion This fascinating catch of fishy facts offers a whole new angle on angling. ISBN 1-86105-919-1

The Gardener's Companion For anyone who has gone in search of flowers, beauty and inspiration. ISBN 1-86105-771-7

The Golfer's Companion From plus fours to six irons, here's where to find the heaven and hell of golf. ISBN 1-86105-834-9

The History of Britain Companion All the oddities, quirks, origins and stories that make our country what it is today. ISBN 1-86105-914-0

The Ideas Companion The stories behind the trademarks, inventions, and brands that we come across every day. ISBN 1-86105-835-7

The Legal Companion From lawmakers to lawbreakers, find out all the quirks and stories behind the legal world. ISBN 1-86105-838-1

The Literary Companion Literary fact and fiction from Rebecca East to Vita Sackville-West. ISBN 1-86105-798-9

The London Companion Explore the history and mystery of the most exciting capital city in the world. ISBN 1-86105-799-7

The Moviegoer's Companion Movies, actors, cinemas and salty popcorn in all their glamorous glory. ISBN 1-86105-797-0

The Politics Companion Great leaders and greater liars of international politics gather round the hustings. ISBN 1-86105-796-2

The Sailing Companion Starboards, stinkpots, raggie and sterns – here's where to find out more. ISBN 1-86105-839-X

The Shakespeare Companion A long, hard look at the man behind the moustache and his plethora of works. ISBN 1-86105-913-2

The Traveller's Companion For anyone who's ever stared at a plane and spent the day dreaming of faraway lands. ISBN 1-86105-773-3

The Walker's Companion Ever laced a sturdy boot and stepped out in search of stimulation? This book is for you. ISBN 1-86105-825-X

The Wildlife Companion Animal amazements and botanical beauties abound in this book of natural need-to-knows. ISBN 1-86105-770-9